Praise for *Let Them Play*

"Jerry Lynch's new book, *Let Them P*̶ ̶ts
parents. As a college coach and ̶
witnessed the craziness of you ̶
even at the collegiate level. The ̶ ̶ ̶ pressure
and anxiety on both the kids and t ̶ ̶ ̶ ry's proven philosophy and lessons have greatly influenced my life — coaching and parenting. He continues to provide me with strategies that help me, my kids at home, and the athletes I work with to build confidence, navigate challenges, and have more fun — as well as with ways to allow me to just let them play."

> — **Jenny Levy**, head coach of the 2013 national champion
> women's lacrosse team at University of North Carolina

"In the midst of a culture in which sports has become a business, Jerry Lynch has written a vital guide to the joy of play, for both parents and children. He illustrates the importance to children of actually being able to *play* sports. He releases parents from the futile task of trying to live their children's lives, releases children from the need to perform for their parents, and allows both parents and children to find the freedom and joy of approaching life with a spirit of play. If we were to heed the wise counsel contained in this book, sports would become fun again, for our children and for us."

> — **William Martin**, author of *The Parent's Tao Te Ching*

"Do you want the children in your life to experience your unconditional love and acceptance? And do you also want them to learn how to succeed and excel? If you want to find true balance and wisdom as a parent, as a coach, and as a human being, this is the book for you."

> — **John Robbins**, author of *Diet for a New America*
> and cofounder of the Food Revolution Network

"Whether you're a parent, coach, or player, you will love *Let Them Play*. It will help you to be more mindful in all your parenting of these young athletes, especially when it comes to offering instruction and advice to your child during a game."

— from the foreword by **Steve Kerr**,
head coach of the Golden State Warriors

"Jerry Lynch is a good friend and professional colleague who has given me much encouragement and wisdom, helping me and my athletes to reach new levels of our potential. With his latest book, *Let Them Play*, Jerry is right there in the midst of the moment, encouraging you to be more mindful along the path. Having been a parent of athletic kids, I wish I had had a copy of this book to guide me through those challenging times with youth sports."

— **Phil Jackson**, author and
eleven-time NBA world champion coach

"Jerry Lynch is a wise and trusted friend who happens to be one of the nation's top authorities on coaching and parenting athletes of all ages. His new book, *Let Them Play*, will help you to inspire and empower your kids to have more joy, fun, and success not just in sports but in the bigger game of life. I have used his services and I love his work."

— **Anson Dorrance**, coach of the twenty-two-time NCAA
champion women's soccer team at University of North Carolina

"If you have a child in sports, you must read *Let Them Play*. It will teach you how to help your kids get the most good out of sports, while avoiding most of the bad. This book is my new blueprint for raising my own happy, healthy athletes, and it should be yours too."

— **John O'Sullivan**, founder of the Changing the Game Project

LET
THEM
PLAY

Also by Jerry Lynch

Thinking Body, Dancing Mind
Mentoring
Working Out, Working Within
Creative Coaching
The Way of the Champion
Spirit of the Dancing Warrior
Coaching with Heart

LET
THEM
PLAY

The Power & Joy
of Mindful
Sports Parenting

JERRY LYNCH

FOREWORD BY
STEVE KERR

New World Library
Novato, California

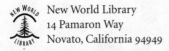

New World Library
14 Pamaron Way
Novato, California 94949

Text design by Tona Pearce Myers

Library of Congress Cataloging-in-Publication Data is available.

First printing, September 2016
ISBN 978-1-60868-434-2
Ebook ISBN 978-1-60868-435-9
Printed in Canada on 100% postconsumer-waste recycled paper

New World Library is proud to be a Gold Certified Environmentally Responsible Publisher. Publisher certification awarded by Green Press Initiative. www.greenpressinitiative.org

10 9 8 7 6 5 4 3 2 1

I dedicate this book to my athletic kids, my Zen masters in residence, who taught me unsolicited mindfulness lessons on the importance of being a good sports parent while I navigated the turbulent waters of youth athletics.

Contents

PART THREE Navigating Uncharted Waters: Lessons for Personal and Athletic Awareness

PART FOUR Code of Conduct: Giving the Game Back to Them

Foreword

Next time you attend a Little League baseball game, try to be mindful of what happens when a young batter comes to the plate. The third-base coach might yell, "Make sure you get a good pitch to hit!" The manager may say from the dugout, "Keep your eye on the ball!" Mom or Dad might be in the stands yelling, "Come on, keep your weight back!" By the time the first pitch comes, the poor kid has a dozen thoughts in his or her head!

The irony, of course, is that while every single person is trying desperately to help, they are all unwittingly making the young batter's job nearly impossible. Like any endeavor in life, hitting a baseball requires practice, focus, and concentration. Who can concentrate with four or five people yelling different tips at the same time?

My point is this: if you want to help your child succeed in sports — or anything else, for that matter — offer your child support, love, and perhaps more than anything, the space to experience and learn on his or her own!

As a lifelong athlete and current coach, it took me a while to understand that lesson. As a kid, I was competitive, emotional, and prone to fits of anger when things didn't go my way. As I got older, I calmed down — to a point. But for many years, even as a professional basketball player, I was a wreck. I would hear fans' jeers, read journalists' jabs, and succumb to an opponent's trash talk. I fashioned myself as poised and fearless, but the truth is I was vulnerable.

I met Jerry Lynch in the midnineties when I was playing for the Chicago Bulls. He was a friend of Phil Jackson, who enjoyed teaching our team the values of balance and mindfulness. Jerry came from the same mind-set when it came to sports and life, and he introduced me to several of his books, including *The Way of the Champion*. As I grew as a player and as a person, I began to understand the power of the mind as it related to my success on the court. There was so much clutter out there, so many ways for my mind to be distracted from the things I needed to do to succeed. I began to train my mind to avoid those distractions through breathing and meditation. And I was inspired by Jerry's books, learning ways to enhance my concentration and really focus my effort on the only thing that mattered — my own play. I realized that my improvement was mostly a by-product of a ton of practice, both on the court and with my own thoughts.

Now that I'm coaching, I have carried that philosophy with me as it relates to my players. Each day, I want to offer them advice and support; a fun, joyful environment; and ultimately, the space to learn on their own. Most of our staff's coaching comes in practice, behind the scenes in our gym in a teaching environment. Once the games start, we try to give our players the freedom and support they need to play a loose, confident style. At that point, it's way too late to try to "teach" something in the heat of battle. Prepare the players and *let them play* — that's our style. They're the ones who do all the work, and they've trained for it all their lives. Other than an occasional nudge or push, the coach's job is to get out of the players' way!

Jerry Lynch shares the same mindful philosophy when it comes to an athlete's growth, and that's one of the reasons we've become friends. He believes in the human spirit, the power of the mind, and learning through experience. Whether you're a parent, coach, or player, you will love *Let Them Play*. It will help you to be more mindful in all your parenting of these young athletes, especially when it comes to offering instruction and advice to your child during a game. Maybe by sitting back, enjoying the game, observing your child in action, and just letting them play — as Jerry's book title suggests — you can help your child learn the game faster and enjoy it more. Just a thought.

— Steve Kerr, head coach, Golden State Warriors

Introduction:
Walking the Path of Wisdom

. Your life is a sacred journey. It is about change, growth, discovery, movement, transformation, continuously expanding your vision of what is possible, stretching your soul, learning to see clearly and deeply, listening to your intuition, taking courageous challenges at every step.... You are on the path, exactly where you are meant to be right now.

— Chinese wisdom

Parenting athletic children is difficult. Actually, I am understating the case. It often can be enigmatic, mysterious, nebulous, confusing, complex, formidable, inconvenient, demanding, burdensome, unmanageable, and at times, a crazy nightmare.

Having said all that, this sacred journey also has the potential to be the most rewarding, mystical, spiritual experience of your life.

As I often tell my parent groups, from the day my first child was born, I realized much to my chagrin that I had to grow up. I now was responsible for another human being's life. And I had no manuals or road maps to guide me. Once my kids were old enough to play sports at the age of six, a new level of chaos was added to our already-turbulent lives. This included attending out-of-town tournaments, getting the kids to and from practice, arranging individual coaching sessions, treating injuries, paying the costs of the more-competitive leagues, and having our weekends filled with athletic and other nonvoluntary activities, like fundraising or working in the snack bar, year round.

As all of this was happening, it quickly became apparent that navigating these turbulent, uncharted waters was a path that would teach me, whether I liked it or not, the deeper, more meaningful, sacred lessons of life — lessons about trust, integrity, patience, respect, acceptance, understanding, giving, generosity, selflessness, gratitude, boundaries, and mostly, unconditional love. My kids demanded that I be present and *mindful*. This wasn't easy, and I was continually made aware of my shortcomings, inconsistencies, and hypocritical behaviors, which was uncomfortable, to say the least. I thought I was an adult, but I often caught myself acting like a child. My behavior forced me to look at myself in the mirror, and I didn't always like what I saw.

While all of this "schooling" initially brought much pain, it eventually showered me with extraordinary joy. My kids became my "Zen masters in residence," and I became "child-wise" as they taught me, without necessarily meaning to, what I needed to know to be a true human being. As parents, we can learn those deep spiritual traits in any context, but the beauty of athletics is that they greatly accelerate the process. A one-hour athletic event presents us with multiple immediate, urgent, and challenging choices about how to act. We learn lessons about parenting that might take a month, a year, or even a lifetime to confront and absorb without sports.

For myself, I felt like I had enrolled in sports parenting school.

I took many tests and experienced many setbacks and mistakes. With my first child, I made at least five thousand mistakes. By the time my fourth child came along, I made only fifty. With each of my children, I became more proficient, learning from my previous setbacks and errors, and this was very satisfying. My mistakes served as my invisible teachers and became gifts of wisdom guiding me along this path to help my kids have a more meaningful relationship with their passion.

In addition, for forty years I have worked in the trenches as a sports psychologist, partnering with hundreds of coaches, championship athletic teams, and thousands of extraordinary athletes, all of whom have taught me so much more than I could teach them about what it takes to be a champion. The wisdom I have gained from the arena of sports continues to deepen every day, and in this book I share those lessons to help you help your athletic child to understand what competition and performance are all about.

Supporting all of my invaluable hands-on learning as a parent and professional sports psychologist, I have garnered much wisdom from various contemplative, cultural philosophies. These have taught me that life works according to natural ways, and I always try to apply these teachings to my sports parenting journey. My philosophical base — my "go-to" anchor and reference point, especially when I struggle or fall off track with my parenting, which I still do from time to time — is a combination of Christian mysticism, Eastern thought, Native American traditions, and Western psychology. I gained much knowledge in these cultural ways from my postdoctoral studies in comparative religion and cross-cultural philosophy. In *Let Them Play*, I integrate these universal systems with my rich professional and parenting experiences as a dad of four athletic children, weaving them into a beautiful tapestry that could be thought of as a "way" or path. In Chinese philosophy, this is called the Tao, which translates as "walking the path of wisdom." I have written this book with this path in mind.

My intention is to provide a useful, easy-to-read, practical manual — one I wish I'd had as a neophyte sports parent — for all adults involved intimately in the world of children's athletics. My aim is to encourage a more conscious level of parenting as well as to help guide you in raising true champions capable of extraordinary performance. I believe that sport is an invaluable training ground that can enable children to learn many valuable lessons, not only about sports, but about life as well.

I have divided the book into four parts. Part 1, "From Craziness to Mindfulness," begins by discussing a certain type of over-involved, hyper-competitive, sports-crazy parent that we have all seen or heard about in youth sports circles. These parents occasionally make the news for their egregious bad behavior in the name of "helping" their child in sports. While these parents are in the minority, they raise issues every parent of a young athlete must wrestle with. Every parent wants their children to succeed, and yet at times our well-meaning efforts to support our children can backfire and instead become detrimental or counterproductive. By retelling these stories, I wish to create awareness so that we can all be more informed. For one thing, we must unite together to assure we maintain safe environments for our kids. Even when we are *not* part of the problem, we *are* part of the solution. But we also must become self-aware of our own attitudes and behaviors. In part 1, I present proven strategies and tools for healthy, mindful parenting of sports children.

In part 2, "Minding the Game, Mending the Mind," I discuss ways to help you and your child be more *mindful* about having fun, that is, minding the game while mending the mind. By "minding the game," I mean that we take care of, care about, and look after the game of sports, which is meant to be fun. Simultaneously, we "mend the mind" by helping to improve and better serve our child in the mental aspects of successful performance. I offer game plans or blueprints for *mindful* awareness that will help your young stars to play sports with less stress, tension, and anxiety — especially anxiety over adult expectations. As a result, children play and perform at higher levels and with more joy and fun. As you become more emotionally and spiritually available for your kids, everyone experiences greater awareness, enthusiasm, passion, and emotional engagement. This mindful approach demonstrates how, quite often, less is more, soft is strong, and loss is gain. Such guidance with heart will enable you to bring your full, complete, loving human self to your sports parenting while embracing athletics as a microcosmic classroom that can teach your kids to grow as people and performers. When this happens, sport becomes more than a fun, dynamic activity for physical, mental, and emotional development; it becomes a bright beacon illuminating the path for success in the bigger game of life.

In part 3, "Navigating Uncharted Waters," I offer many specific, mindful ways and insightful, time-honored strategies for guiding children with heart and relevance. Almost always, as parents, we mean well even when we make mistakes. If we, armed and fortified with a sense of mindful optimism, set our intention to learn from any mistakes and practice healthy sports parenting, we can open a whole new world for ourselves and our spirited young stars. In this part, I provide practices for creating a mindful meditative approach to sports parenting, and I discuss your purpose and role in the process. I will help you navigate many of the treacherous waters of youth athletics, such as recruiting, tryouts, getting cut, readiness, sportsmanship, quitting, and more.

Finally, in part 4, "Code of Conduct," I provide exactly that, code-of-conduct guidelines for sports parents. They begin with the imperative that parents must give the game back to the children. After all, sports are "child's play." Let children have a ball, playing just as they are and having fun in the moment. Such affirmative expressions serve as mindful guides to help us navigate the path of healthy conduct. In the big picture, all we need to do, as the book title states, is to *let them play*.

Throughout the book, I've also included quotes from a variety of thinkers, writers, and athletes that I use consistently in my work with coaches, athletes, and parents. The quotes that are attributed to "Chinese wisdom" are my interpretation of certain passages from classic Chinese books, like the *Tao Te Ching*, the *I Ching*, *The Art of War*, and several other tomes. I have rephrased this ancient wisdom to emphasize its relevance for modern sports.

It goes without saying that we love our kids. Yet as I have discovered in my own parenting, it's easy to lose touch with what is best for our kids and to unintentionally superimpose our needs upon them rather than listen to what they need and better understand their struggles. When our children fail, lose, drop out, get cut, and have setbacks, we as parents can feel like failures, like we've let them down when they don't make it. Parents are usually only as happy as their unhappiest child. We have a tendency to internalize their shortcomings and problems as our doing. However, if we just listen and offer suggestions, our children will have the opportunity to decide what is best for themselves in many situations, and you will be a happier, more effective parent.

In part 4, the precepts I offer are not for indoctrination, but for contemplation. These ideas are capable of creating radical changes not just in our parenting styles but in our attitudes and beliefs. Their aim is to help our children develop as total athletes and full human beings, capable of excellence and extraordinary performance.

When it comes to parenting, sports, and coaching, I am neither a purist nor a traditionalist. I try to avoid dogma. Rather, I consider myself a student applying the wisdom learned from those who taught me well. I am like a conduit, putting my spin on the wisdom of others as I teach practical methods for approaching sports and the bigger game of life. Scholar Huston Smith said he considered himself like the hole in a flute where the breath of others comes through. I am that "hole."

I wrote this book to help you improve and optimize the effectiveness of your parenting and coaching skill set. No doubt, there are certain things you already do very well, and other things that could be improved. This is true for all of us. From time to time, we all need to add to our skills and expand our repertoire to help us raise our levels of effectiveness. Sometimes we may feel stagnant, stuck, or on a plateau. If this is you, read this book with the commitment to change what isn't working. Hopefully, this will be just what you need to nudge yourself along the path of a more conscious, *mindful* approach to children's sports and parenting.

This book encourages you to be more respectful and sensitive to your athletic kids' needs, which is how we gain their loyalty, love, cooperation, and appreciation. Taking this path, you can also expect to become more flexible and balanced in your own life. A natural by-product of instilling these philosophies and attitudes in your kids is that you, yourself, become the change you want to see in them.

Many parents believe that we, as teachers, need to know everything. That's too much to expect of ourselves. Wise parents know they don't have all the answers, which is the attitude we need to adopt before we can learn. Consider the classic Zen story about the pompous professor who visits the Zen master to learn about Buddhism. The Zen master invites the professor for tea, and as he pours the tea, the master keeps pouring until the cup is overflowing. The professor protests that this is making a mess, not teaching, and the master gently explains, "Exactly. Your knowledge is already spilling over, so how can I offer you any more?"

It feels good to be an "empty cup." Practice remaining open and empty to receive new ways to guide your kids. In fact, when I strive to appear less knowledgeable than I am, I commit fewer errors and mistakes, since I feel less pressure to live up to expectations or to be someone I am not.

If you remain open and receptive on this path, follow your intuition, and do what feels right, this parent-child dance with sports will lead to much wisdom and you will become a more effective sports parent. Be an open vessel, fill up with wisdom, and enjoy this dance. Consider the advice of Buddha:

> Know well what leads you forward and what holds you back,
> and walk the path that leads to wisdom.

PART ONE

From Craziness to Mindfulness

Sports Parenting Nightmare

Too much interference will backfire. Constant interventions spoil the child. Conscious guidance is delicate; it cannot be forced. Force, pushing, or control will cost you the trust of your child. Parents who guide this way think they're helping progress when, actually, they are contributing to a senseless world and unconsciously obstructing the path.

— Chinese wisdom

W hen I look back on the days of my glorious athletic childhood, it appears as though my uneducated parents (my dad only made it to the eighth grade) were, indeed, quite wise in their understandable sea of ignorance. I never experienced "too much interference" from them. There were no "constant interventions" to hamper my progress in athletics. During summer vacations, all the kids in my Brooklyn neighborhood would religiously congregate at the local schoolyard every day from eight in the morning to nine at night to play stickball, baseball, handball, boxball, football, basketball, "off-the-wall" ball, and whatever other ball we could drum up on our own. We had a "ball." We created games, chose sides, kept score, played for sodas, argued, fought, and battled. Without adults to interfere, we solved our

differences and quickly resumed our activities. No whining, no
drama, no worries...it was all good. So good, in fact, that we all
became amazing athletes in multiple sports (I played three sports
in high school), several of us going on to compete collegiately,
nationally, and at the professional level.

Those were the "good old days" when first base was a kid's
hat, second was a cardboard box top, third base a T-shirt, and
home plate a square of wood. Yet without coaches or parents and
fancy gear, we developed character, pride, courage, tenacity, fear-
lessness, respect, and all the skills and characteristics required to
have fun, play well, compete with the hearts of warriors, and develop the tools necessary to go the distance, not just in sport but
in all of life.

Why are sports so different today? We seem to have gone to
the opposite extreme, so much so that we are often "unconsciously
obstructing the path." Granted, even in the good old days, a little
input from our "hands-off" parents would have been nice — to
have them appear occasionally at an important game or simply
to ask, "How did it go? How was it?" Today, however, we are experiencing a deluge of parental intervention, almost to the point
where one wonders whether kids are playing for themselves or
for the entertainment of their parents, who often live vicariously
through their kids' achievements. Sports have shifted to become a
more parent-centric activity, and with this has come a myriad of
problems. At the extreme, it encourages senseless, irrational behavior and ultimately hinders the process and the good-natured
intentions that most parents have for their children.

A dear friend, Jenny Levy, head coach of women's lacrosse at
the University of North Carolina, summed it up beautifully in a

recent email to me: "We are fully involved in the soccer/lacrosse parent world with our own kids — I feel the parents are driving a train from the back. Yikes! Perspective has been lost and everything is results driven. The club sports organizations are just trying to make money — so they sell a dream to a kid and parents — be the best, get a scholarship to college, and so on. The wear and tear on kids' bodies, the lack of family time during the week and weekends, make for complete family chaos and insanity. It's a nightmare."

This nightmare is exemplified by a plethora of incidents in recent years that seem surreal yet have actually taken place, indicating how "out of control" youth sports have become. Several years ago, a *Sports Illustrated* special report described the rising tide of crazy adult behaviors connected to youth sports, and it mentioned the following:

- In Swiftwater, Pennsylvania, police had to be called to stop a fight between fifty parents and players who went at one another following a football game involving eleven- to thirteen-year-olds.
- Following a Little League game in Sacramento, California, a coach beat up the manager of the opposing team.
- A policeman in Pennsylvania gave two dollars to a ten-year-old pitcher to hit a batter with a fastball.
- A soccer dad in Ohio was charged with assault after he punched a fourteen-year-old boy for doing something he did not like.
- A youth baseball coach in Florida broke an umpire's jaw when the umpire was throwing the coach out of the game.

- Two thousand youth-league parents in Florida were required to sign a pledge to behave themselves at games.

- In Cleveland, Ohio, a soccer league held a "silent Sunday" in which parents were under strict orders not to yell instructions to kids, not to question officials, and not to cheer at all.

While these incidents happened several years ago, the craziness has not subsided. In 2014, the Little League World Series was marred by a scandal involving ineligible players. Chicago's Jackie Robinson West team advanced to the championship game (which it lost to South Korea), but afterward all its wins were vacated, or disallowed, when it was learned that some of its players illegally lived outside assigned geographical boundaries, violating residency rules. The Chicago team had secretly expanded league boundaries to recruit star players. The organization's manager and district administrator were removed for this violation.

Today, youth athletics are rigidly organized, which greatly contributes to the sports parenting nightmare we are experiencing. This creates unbearable fear, anxiety, and stress for young athletes, cutting into the fun and thrill of learning new skills and undermining the satisfaction of sports accomplishments. Reports of vociferous, critical, obnoxious, meddling, and aggressive parents are now commonplace, an alarming trend in youth athletics that borders on insanity. What is being lost is the spirit of childhood and the joy of family life. Kids don't pal around and hang out. Youth sports are filled with constant pressure and real-world consequences. Forgotten in the process is that sports are supposed to be fun, and the emphasis on effort, skill development, and participation is often lost.

The Lure of Reaching the Pros

Anyone who has recently been to a youth athletic event can testify that it has become more parent-centric over the years. For what it's worth, one of the more astonishing statistics circulating in youth sports circles is that there are 33 million kids in athletics today between the ages of five and seventeen (assuming each child has two parents, that means up to 99 million people are involved). Yet by the age of thirteen, 75 percent of kids drop out of organized sports. While there are several reasons for this mass exodus, a major cause happens to be "over the top" parents, whose involvement, expectations, and pressure to excel drive kids to quit.

How crazy is this? Unfortunately, such unintentional negative interference by parents can cause children to abandon a healthy activity, one that often leads youth away from drug and alcohol abuse, criminal involvement, teen pregnancy, and a host of other deleterious activities. Many young athletes become mentally, emotionally, and spiritually fried by the constant competitive pressure, which includes the overwhelming obsession to win, to gain external recognition, to attain perfection, to fulfill unrealistic expectations, and to measure self-worth solely by results and outcomes. Further, overzealous parents can become seduced by the possibility of their daughter or son getting on an athletic scholarship track and catching the next train to Stanford.

I have talked with parents who are frantic and fearful about their kid's future, and many see sports as their child's ticket to success. Yet the statistical chances of a kid getting a college athletic scholarship are very small. Parents can also buy in to the notion that if they don't intervene and involve themselves in their kid's game, they are bad parents, letting their little stars down. If they don't get involved, they feel guilty, scared, and empty. If their kids get cut, quit the team, or perform poorly, the parents feel that it's their fault. If kids don't recover emotionally from failure in sports, either quickly or well, parents can feel responsible for this, too.

Of course, no one is a bad parent for wanting their kid to get into Stanford, and we aren't wrong to want our kids to be successful at sports. On the other hand, being a successful sports parent isn't about doing and giving up everything for sports: you don't have to pay out boatloads of money for travel teams, give up your entire weekends to competitive events, suspend your vacations, and sell your home to afford the extra expense. What a child achieves in athletics is no indication of whether the parents are doing a good job or not. A parent's intentions are not usually the main problem, since we all love our kids and want the best for them. My goal in this book is to help you channel those intentions so you do the *right thing*. And the first thing we must all learn is how to free ourselves so we can step away, get out of the way, and simply *let them play*.

I believe that when we give the game back to our children we demonstrate the highest level of love for these great young spirits. When I ask kids why they play sports, they almost never mention scholarships, going pro, or winning a championship. They usually couldn't care less about such lofty goals. They want to have fun, feel challenged, and make friends. Kids crave enjoyment, balanced lives, and even the opportunity to play multiple sports. Have we as parents become trapped and simply lost sight of their innocent goals? I often ask kids, "How can your parents help you in sports?" They unanimously respond, "They need to listen to us and know we want to have fun and just play."

It's easy to get caught in this sports parent trap and not listen to our kids or what we intuitively know to be the right thing. Perhaps you have noticed, for example, how youth sports have steadily become big business. Someone is making good money from willing parents. You may feel forced to "go along with the program" and get your kids on board with the more competitive leagues, requiring the family to shell out tons of money — all on the hope or promise that your children might become shining professional stars someday. Of course, a few do, but the percentage who "make it big" is so infinitely small that it's hardly worth even considering. Even understanding this, you may find yourself becoming uncertain, nervous, tense, and stressed, and the thought of doing the right thing gets lost in the process. I have a continuous flow of parents in my practice, neophytes to this strange sports scene, who are looking for guidance through such turbulence. Rather than listening to or trusting their children, they are trying to push, force, or manage the process. They are fearful of making a wrong decision. I reassure them to listen to their gut and follow their hearts, to sense what they intuitively feel is the right thing to do. They are good parents with good intentions, yet they need to learn how to navigate these uncharted, often-turbulent waters of sports parenting.

Everyone's Been There, Everyone's Involved

As the father of four athletic kids, I have witnessed many nightmare-parent scenarios. Overzealous adults show up every Saturday at the soccer field. But I understand why parents act this way because, as embarrassing as it is for me to think about it, I had to learn through my own foolish mistakes. As a parent of young athletes, I sometimes found myself being part of the problem. I often failed to do the right thing. On several occasions, I shouted at a referee or official. I even argued with other parents about how their kid didn't deserve more minutes. I once confronted a coach about why my kid wasn't playing. Perhaps it was my "Brooklyn fight" coming out. Thankfully, my kids called me on these incidents, and because of their efforts, I turned myself around quickly. I had good intentions but exhibited poor behavior.

Parents can engage in all sorts of bad behavior through their desire to defend their kids and see them succeed. I have witnessed parents advise their child to fight back, shoulder the opponent, "run over him," and just get that killer instinct going so they measure up. I've seen coaches playing only the best lineups until the win is assured, and only then do any other players get to play. Some parents applaud this strategy, while others are offended by it.

Even when we try to be supportive, we can overdo it. I once learned that the mother of a child on my son's soccer team paid her son five dollars for each goal scored and one dollar for each assist. The boy gleefully told my son that he had earned sixteen dollars for his performance after one game. However, this seemingly innocent gesture is ultimately damaging to youngsters and certainly to the purpose of team play. External reward systems send the wrong message: motivation to play sports becomes monetary and selfish rather than for the joy and excitement of team play. For parents, this is not doing the right thing. It contradicts the essence of sport, which was clearly articulated by the leader of the Olympic Movement, Pierre de Coubertin, at the opening of the 1908 Olympic Games in London: "The most important thing in the Olympic Games is not to win, but to take part."

Most damaging of all, of course, is when parents criticize and belittle their own children over a poor performance, particularly in front of others. At a Little League baseball game, I once witnessed a father shout at his nine-year-old son: "You're embarrassing me. You do that again and I'll put you in the outfield.... Clumsy klutz, what's wrong with you? You stink! Keep that up and you won't play on this team."

These shocking words cut deeply into the spirit of the innocent boy, thoroughly humiliating him in the presence of his friends. Yet just as outrageous was the quiet demeanor of other onlooking adults during such a disgraceful tirade; no one reacted or spoke up for this boy. This is not doing the right thing. This parent had created an emotionally unsafe environment that affected all the kids. Unfortunately, for this particular child, such unacceptance and disrespect could permanently extinguish his passion for sport and scar his self-esteem. How many other careers of budding athletes have been curtailed by overbearing parents?

In all these ways, caring parents can turn into overzealous, overbearing parents who focus on winning and athletic achievements at the expense of the simple joys of participation in sports. When this happens, as my dear friend and colleague John O'Sullivan so eloquently says, "You run the race to nowhere where kids do not become better athletes. They become bitter athletes who get injured, burn out, and quit sports altogether."

How do we avoid this? In a word, by being *mindful*. In the next section, I talk about mindfulness and how it can help us be better sports parents for our little stars.

The Mindful Way

Mindfulness is simply being aware of what is happening right now without wishing it were different; enjoying the pleasant without holding on when it changes (which it will); being with the unpleasant without fearing it will always be this way (which it won't).

— James Baraz, *Awakening Joy*

The notion of mindfulness is closely aligned with the roots of ancient Buddhist teaching. I use it as a powerful way to practice being awake and aware of thoughts and actions as they occur in the present moment. Through this very simple practice, you improve self-awareness, so in any moment, you know what you are doing, how you are doing it, and why, while understanding how your actions influence your kids in a profound way.

I see sports parenting as one of the greatest environments to practice mindfulness. Its essence is universal. You need not be a Zen Buddhist monk practicing *zazen* (sitting meditation) on a mountaintop to practice being aware and present. Mindfulness has actually become profoundly relevant in mainstream America. It's embraced by hospitals helping patients to heal, military groups wanting to focus, educational systems hoping to facilitate learning, musicians wishing to be more present, and actors trying to stay in the moment. It can also be used by you, a sports parent looking to enjoy the experience of your children having fun and being happy in real time. Say good-bye to multitasking and using devices at your kid's games, and welcome the rapture of the present moment as you do the right thing long enough to feel its fullness.

Mindfulness is about waking up to the present moment to experience the vitality of life. The aim isn't to do this once but on a consistent basis. It can help you to see clearly and act more appropriately when it comes to being the best sports parent for your child. The Chinese symbols for *mindfulness* translate as "music from the heart as we become fully awakened with all of our sensory perceptions." Mindfulness has strong implications for our actions, words, and decisions in all areas of our lives. Buddhism teaches that the "monkey mind" is the scattered focus of everyday life, but this can be tamed through a more mindful approach so our focus remains in the here and now.

The most well-recognized Western definition of mindfulness comes from one of the most prominent, best-known teachers of the concept — Jon Kabat-Zinn. He states that mindfulness is "paying attention in a particular way, on purpose, in the present moment." For sports parents like us, mindfulness becomes the art and act of simply watching our kids play and loving their joy, happiness, and ups and downs every minute we are present at their events. It is seeing and experiencing our kids as spirited beings, not athletic doings. Being mindful is easy, yet we often forget and need a gentle reminder to not get caught up in the surrounding chatter and insanity. Hopefully, this book can serve as your personal mindfulness coach, helping you get back on track and become the conscious, awake, and attentive parent that your kids need. Mindfulness is truly about waking up and living harmoniously without judgment in concert with the world around you. Being mindful is your commitment to kick your relationship up a few notches with your kids, your family, and the sports you experience. It will also help you to discover a healthier, stronger relationship with yourself. Rather than taking life for granted, you will start to take life gratefully, focusing on all you have already been given. In the words of the Chinese sage Lao Tzu, being mindful helps you to "rejoice in the way things are; when you realize that nothing is lacking, the whole world belongs to you."

Becoming more mindful puts you more in touch with the richness of what athletics offer for your kids, as well as with the profound, soulful process of conscious parenting and living. It can help you to see and feel more clearly, deeply, and joyfully. It is a process independent of outcomes or results, as it focuses on all the essential little things you can do in this very moment. This awakeness is not only for this moment, but it helps you be aware of important future events, so that you may pay attention and take positive action, all under the guise of being mindful.

Ultimately, mindfulness is a practice, not an end. There is no path to mindfulness; mindfulness is the path, the practice of being in this moment. In the words of Thich Nhat Hanh, "Life is available only in the present moment." I call this place "the still point within."

The Still Point Within

Do you have the patience to wait till your mind settles and the water is clear? Can you remain unmoving till the right action arises by itself?

— Lao Tzu

The practice of meditation, which I call "the still point within," is a skill that, when developed, can impact not just your sports parenting but your entire life. In this fast-paced, often-turbulent world, meditation helps you to slow things down and create an inner world where mindfulness can blossom, and this will enable you to use the strategies and tools offered in this book on a more consistent basis. As with mindfulness, the concept of meditation has become mainstream, and it is used by others in all walks of life.

In his coaching days, Phil Jackson, an eleven-time NBA world champion coach, designated a room in the team's training facility as the "warrior room," a place where athletes could meditate prior to practice or a game to help still their minds, relax their bodies, and focus on the upcoming tasks at hand. I have trained athletes and sports teams over the past forty years to use meditation as a preparation for their performances in practice and competitive events. They all claim it has benefited them greatly. In my personal life, I have a daily practice that helps me to access my still point, so I can be more conscious, awake, relaxed, calm, and aware of how I want to be, to act, and to perform.

According to ancient Taoist thought, it is practically impossible to reach our full human capacity without daily periods of silence, retreat, and reflection. In Chinese, the expression *shang shan* suggests ascending to the mountaintop in order to escape the chaos below. The peak provides peace and clarity of thought as you get "on top of things" in life. The mountaintop is a sanctuary where you can return to achieve your still point, a sacred place of harmony, balance, and ease. Isn't this what we all need, perhaps crave, when things around us get out of control in the world of youth sports?

While I believe strongly in the benefits of meditation, it is obviously not a prerequisite for being a good, successful sports parent. However, if you haven't already, I encourage you to try it. You may find value in the process, and the meditation style I describe here is simple and user friendly. I suggest a fifteen-minute session, but at first, if you only do five minutes or even one minute of meditation, that will be useful. That alone will train you to stop, look, and listen to your inner voice for wisdom and direction when it comes to any aspect of personal performance. Of course, you can teach your child how to meditate, but I suggest you simply teach by example with this. That's how our kids seem to learn best…by observing the changes they see in our behaviors and actions.

The version of meditation that I teach is a simple variation of a 2,500-year-old form of Buddhist meditation called Vipassana meditation, a Pali word meaning *insight*. It relies on your ability to focus on your natural breathing patterns as you sit quietly in the absence of distraction. This helps to clear the mind and create an in-the-moment experience. Sophisticated in its simplicity, this meditation does require consistency of practice, like any skill. It will help you to focus your attention and awareness in the moment and become more mindful in the here and now.

To begin, get comfortable sitting in a chair or on the floor where you can be free of distraction or noise. Close your eyes to better concentrate and focus on the natural movement of your breath. See and feel your breath. On the in-breath, imagine your hand pulling the breath up from the heart, up through your neck, to the crown of your head. Then feel the out-breath, and imagine gently pushing the breath back down with your hand to the heart. Repeat this process for several breaths. If your mind wanders, that is natural. Just quietly say inside, "Wandering, come back," and then immediately focus again on the pattern of your breathing. You can do this for three, five, ten, or more minutes — for as long as you'd like. This creates a still point inside, a place of inner calm, clarity, peace, and quiet, which becomes the basis for feeling mindful and knowing what demonstrates right action. This is key to maintaining harmony, alliance, and focus for being a mindful sports parent.

One variation I suggest is, after watching your breath for as many minutes as you'd like, visualize how you want to be as a parent to your athletic child, using all the suggestions, strategies, and ideas within this book. This will serve as your rehearsal for performing the kinds of actions necessary to be most effective. When you strengthen the mind in this way through meditation, your actions and behaviors in life gradually shift and impact the way you parent and guide your child. This method also enables you to take a good look at yourself and make the appropriate changes in how you accomplish this most important life goal, raising happy, successful kids in sports.

Of course, meditation practice is like physical training; it is exercise for the mind. Such exercise helps you to develop greater mental and emotional strength. Well-conducted scientific studies have demonstrated that after only eight weeks of meditation practice, participants can experience much lower levels of anxiety, higher levels of performance, a significant rise in positive emotions, and more happiness.

Here are some Asian thoughts that may encourage you to dive into the world of meditation: "If you know the art of breathing, you have the strength, wisdom, and courage of ten tigers. The quiet, focused mind can pierce through stone."

Now let's look at how to use mindfulness and meditation to help create a safe, fun environment for our kids through the Buddhist concept of right action.

A Basis for Right Action

The basis of right action is to do everything in mindfulness.

— Thich Nhat Hanh

For me, an important aspect of mindfulness is a concept called *right action* — which is the fourth aspect of the Buddhist eightfold path. Right action is an important step for cultivating a mindful, safe sports environment where our kids can flourish. While "right action" evokes various kinds of work, in the Buddhist sense, it connotes acting in harmony with all things in a mindful way. It is acting with integrity, caring, respect, trust, and kindness. In the context of youth sports, it means demonstrating an attitude of service and giving youngsters what they truly need to succeed and have fun. We can start by giving the game back to them and letting them play.

From my experience as a dad and as a professional in the arena of youth sports, I find that the most effective way to parent young athletes is with compassion and kindness, where one works *with* others, not *over* them. Respecting young athletes first as people is a prime example of right action. A child's performance in any arena of his or her life skyrockets in such a respectful, mindful environment.

Here is a story about a mindful parent demonstrating right action during a crucial baseball playoff game for the league championship. In the last inning with the score tied, two out, and the opponents in scoring position, a parent's son committed a costly error on a routine ground ball that should have been the third out. A run scored, and the team's hopes for the crown went up in smoke. The boy's father was also the team's coach, and once the game ended, he walked onto the field to comfort and embrace his son as the boy cried profusely. How do you think this athlete felt after such emotional support from his compassionate parent? What message was this father sending to his son and to the rest of his team? What effect do you think this conscious, mindful approach had on the boy's future athletic performance? How did everyone feel about the father's right action?

Right action demands that you cultivate a mindful environment of integrity by nurturing greatness in all kids involved in sports. You must learn how to guard the spirit and passion of those you parent, helping your kids to discover the goodness within themselves and empowering them with the notion that they are, indeed, great warriors who are capable of accomplishing their dreams.

Such an approach is a delicate process. It can't be forced. Kids need permission to "fly" when ready, and this sports parenting approach is the key to helping them to move forward when it's safe.

Even then, children won't always succeed, but when all is said and done, if they are nurtured in this way, they will believe that what they accomplish, they have done themselves (which they have).

Right action requires that you enthusiastically communicate to athletic children your belief in their abilities, and as a result, their confidence levels rise. Such validation and affirmation promotes self-reliance and a sense of calm, and it reduces fear about pending performances. I often say to my kids and other young athletes, "I really believe in you," and when I say this, I watch their faces light up.

By creating a mindful, loving, compassionate environment through conscious right action, you give young athletes the chance to step out and risk failure, knowing that setbacks are lessons to help them learn and improve. You should never be afraid to disclose your own failures and how you use them for positive opportunities to raise your own performance levels. One afternoon, my twenty-seven-year-old son was watching me write this book, and I took a moment to tell him how fortunate I felt. Because I'd suffered nine rejections of my original proposal, I learned what I had to do to get the book published, did the work, and wound up having three publishers interested after all those setbacks. Disclosing this made an impression on him. The message he got was that rejection doesn't mean failure and that patience, persistence, and perseverance pay off.

In such a mindful environment, your children can expect to feel free, positive, energetic, and joyful and to possess a strong sense of self-worth. They can count on their spirits being nurtured by the "air of the early dawn," the cool, clean, pure feeling of soft drops of dew, uncontaminated by the pollution of the traditional approach to athletics. This is an environment that is truly liberating for a child — physically, emotionally, mentally, and spiritually — one where continued growth and expansion are not only possible, but probable.

Emphasize personal improvement as a process, and stress participation and quality of play over victory and outcome. True victory is the inevitable result of such a process. Participation is fun, healthy, and exciting, and it enables all to utilize their full range of possibilities. Parenting in this way provides your precious kids with the opportunity to taste what it's like to be a well-respected and trusted person, not just a performance machine.

To guide like this means forgoing the imposition of an adult's or parent's agenda upon these great spirits. Authoritative, hard-nosed, rigid, and inflexible approaches defeat the purpose. Winning should not be the only criteria for success. Self-worth and having fun are more important than the outcome of a game. Kids are not in sport for the sake of their parents. What's important for kids is the connection, the bonding, the camaraderie, and working as a team together to succeed. When this happens, kids learn to connect with something larger than themselves and win the invisible game of life, which is unrelated to the scoreboard. When this happens, each child can become a champion in his or her own right, on his or her own terms. This is all attainable when you cultivate a mindful environment and give the game back to them. That is right action.

The magic of sport can influence a significant portion of a child's physical and emotional development for years to come. When we parent with this belief, we take positive steps to prepare our children to face challenges through competitive situations.

These include learning how to fail, how to succeed, how to overcome self-doubt, how to get stronger mentally and emotionally, and how to develop selflessness. Learning how to navigate these bigger life issues through sport is the focus of the rest of the book.

According to an ancient Sanskrit proverb, "Where there is right action, there is victory." You can apply these and other lessons from this book to preserve what your kids deserve: the ability to enjoy and have fun while developing and testing their newfound skills. For the child, sports then become a gift of enrichment, one that will endure for a lifetime of fun and success.

I believe that as parents we all can benefit in our own lives from these practical strategies of a more conscious, mindful approach. I believe that there is always room to improve our parenting game, and that now is always the right time to do so.

To help prime the pump and keep you focused on creating a thriving, vibrant environment of right action for your athletes, I invite you to recite the following affirmation of heart and compassion for your child. This affirmation is something I created after reading a statement by Rudolf Steiner about his philosophy of teaching, which is the basis of the Waldorf school system. Place it on a placard and hang it in a place that is visible to you on a daily basis. If taken to heart, this affirmation will improve not just your parenting style but also the lives of your children, as you guide them in remarkable, inspiring, and empowering ways.

> Regard the athletes you parent in awe; guide, coach, and serve them in love. Cultivate and teach in a mindful environment, so that they grow with spirit and joy into something extraordinary.

PART TWO

Minding the Game, Mending the Mind

Lessons for Fun and Success in Sports

Be a Champion Now

The vision of a champion is bent over, drenched in sweat, at the point of exhaustion, when nobody else is looking.

— Anson Dorrance

I do know this. Anyone can be a champion, whether they are Steph Curry of the Golden State Warriors, the janitor of your child's elementary school, a grocery store clerk, a local park ranger, or the second-string quarterback on your peewee football team. Being a champion is about practicing the habits and ways of a champion and demonstrating such traits, qualities, and characteristics on a consistent basis. It happens when one becomes dedicated to exploring the unlimited boundaries of one's full human potential in sports and life. Anson Dorrance, in his quote above, sums up this process.

Over the past twenty-five years of my forty-year career in sports, I have had the fortune of being intimately involved with thirty-six national championship teams as well as hundreds of individual national champions. These awesome experiences have taught me everything I know about being a *champion now*. Indeed, I titled one of my twelve books *The Way of the Champion*, and it was so popular that I renamed my business, website, and email address after it. If you'd like to encourage, inspire, and empower your athletic child to live life as a champion, then you yourself need to model such behaviors, demonstrating the correct attitudes and using the right language. If you do, your child's spirit will marinate in the process, and both directly and by osmosis, your child will begin to act like a champion in sports and in life.

What do I know about being a champion? Fasten your seatbelts, because here is what I've learned about what it means to have the "right stuff."

A champion is anyone who

- is a fierce competitor fighting the inner battles of fear, frustration, fatigue, and self-doubt.
- demonstrates courage, determination, persistence, and perseverance.
- strives for positive results yet enjoys the process.
- takes risks to improve, knowing that if failure happens, it is an opportunity to learn and improve on the road of self-discovery.
- focuses on consistent practice and preparation, putting in the work so that the possibility of favorable outcomes and results increases.
- displays a strong work ethic to do whatever it takes to shine.

- understands that winning is a process, not an outcome, something that happens when you win the inner battles over fear and fatigue.
- is willing to sacrifice and suffer to get the job done.
- sees an opponent as a partner who helps push him or her to greater heights.
- knows that outcomes cannot be controlled and focuses on mastering what can be controlled, like doing all the little things, having a strong work ethic, and ensuring proper preparation.
- understands that winning is the willingness to do your best in order to demonstrate your best on a consistent basis.
- realizes the importance of integrity, responsibility, respect, accountability, courage, fortitude, and commitment.
- embraces adversity as an opportunity to grow.
- understands how less is more, soft is strong, and loss is gain.
- practices being selfless and giving to others rather than being concerned about getting.

Participating in athletics is not necessary to be a champion. Anyone in any walk of life can practice the traits of a champion and join that arena. For instance, I will always remember the dedication, sacrifice, suffering, courage, patience, fortitude, determination, and bravery exhibited by my wife, Jan, during the home births of our children. I thought I had experienced grueling pain while running marathons, but this was little compared to the remarkable, valiant efforts of my wife, which I witnessed firsthand, during childbirth. Her preparation and training for those sacred events were akin to the focus of all great championship athletes. Her champion-like mind-set continues to this day: in her work as a physician, as a runner, and as the mom of four challenging, vibrant, and at times very demanding kids. Jan lives the way of the champion.

We don't become champions when we win some external reward — when we cross the finish line first or score the winning goal in the championship game. We become champions when we take the profound, inner, mindful path and succeed against our internal challenges, when we defeat the opponent within, fighting against the demons of fear, failure, fatigue, frustration, and self-doubt. To defeat these opponents, we use the spiritual weapons of the heart. When you practice the "stuff" of champions, and help your children to do so, you and your children will become *champions now*. You will live a life of substance and spirit and be true winners in everything you do.

Beacons in the Night

It is good to have an end to journey toward; but it is the journey
that matters in the end.

— Ernest Hemingway

Rather than see goals as a destination to arrive at, I suggest
that you embrace them as awesome guides, like flashing
beacons on the horizon of the athletic journey. Their function is
to simply keep you on track during this rewarding and exciting
path of sports. Such beacons flash in the distance, encouraging
intentional, purposeful, mindful movement in the direction of
extraordinary performance.

For many athletes, the goal becomes the reason to be, the
end-all, which creates enormous pressure and anxiety. They feel
they must achieve results, since they measure their self-worth by
whether or not the goals are attained.

I am presently working with an Olympic athlete who is one
of the top three in her sport in this country. Only two make the

US Olympic team, unfortunately, so this adds pressure to an already pressurized situation. This athlete told me she doesn't want to set a goal of making the team because it would exacerbate the tension, and it would be a huge disappointment if she failed to reach her goal.

First of all, I told her that no one ever died from disappointment, but you may have to live with regret if you don't "go the distance" and do all you can to position yourself for a favorable outcome. I suggested that she state her goal this way: "I am an elite athlete and strong contender for the US Olympic Team. I medal in my event." Then I told her to use this affirmation as a "coach" or guide to keep her on track. I asked her what needed to be done each day to help her stay on track and keep her feet pointed in this direction. In other words, the goal is the motivation that directs daily performance; you use it to focus on what you need to do today. By so doing, this athlete's mind shifted from uncontrollable outcomes to the controllable process of daily growth, expansion, and improvement. As I explained to her, you can dream about winning, but you must focus on all the little "essential absolutes" that position you for extraordinary performance. She loved this approach and is excited about the possibilities.

The key to successful goals is to remember never to measure your self-worth by outcomes. Gauge your worth on your diligent preparation and your awesome work ethic; focus on one day at a time and enjoy the process. When I was still a competitive runner, I never considered the real prize winning a marathon; it was the exciting, dynamic health program I followed for the three months prior to each race. My reward was the process leading up to the event.

Help your athletic child embrace goals in this same way. This is a counterintuitive way to think in our society, but then, so is so much of what I teach in this book. The champion athletes I have worked with embrace this outside-the-box approach, and their extraordinary performance is a testimony to its validity and power. Remember: If your child shoots for the moon and misses, your child will still be one of the stars. Your child will be further along than if he or she had not set such lofty goals. As a sports parent, do two things with your child's goals. First, encourage your kid to stretch. And second, be realistic with what can be accomplished. Rubber bands stretch, but if they stretch too much, they will break. Your guidance here is so important. Apply this idea to your own exciting life and show your child how it works for you.

Semper Confidere

> Your opponent's greatest advantage is your lack of confidence in yourself.
>
> — Chinese wisdom

One of the more consistent issues that parents are concerned about is their child's loss of confidence. A parent once approached me who wanted my help to restore the confidence of his seven-year-old soccer athlete. I knew without further questioning that this young girl was not having fun playing ball because some adult, either a parent or a coach, was overly concerned about outcomes and results. How silly and how sad at the same time. It's silly that such a young child would be asked to achieve anything but having fun, and it's sad how hurtful the impact of misplaced expectations to win can be. The solution was simple: I told the father, in essence, to *let her play*, to restore fun and enjoyment and being with friends as the main reasons for her to be on the soccer team.

However, older youths often put pressure on themselves, and any child can get "performance anxiety" that undermines their confidence when game time rolls around. Here's a quick, sure way to help child athletes handle their nerves and improve their performance at the same time.

Semper confidere is the Latin expression for "always confident." This is the goal most athletes, young or old, strive for. However, when an athlete shows up to win an event or to have a certain result, he or she will get tight, tense, or tentative because outcomes and results cannot be controlled. When feeling stressed like this, you automatically lose confidence and self-doubt rises. When confidence is lost, performance always suffers. This is exactly what happens when taking a final exam, giving a talk, interviewing for a job, or asking someone out on a date. Since you can't control results, you get nervous, and this jeopardizes the very outcomes you are nervous about.

Explain this to your child, and when game time arrives, encourage your child to focus on what he or she *can* control, that is, all the little essentials that go into playing well. Focus on everything they've been practicing. In basketball, these controllables might be crashing the boards, boxing out, diving for the loose ball, and sprinting back to play tough defense. Since you can control these, you will begin to feel relaxed, calm, and focused. When this happens, your confidence rises and self-doubt disappears. This is when performance blossoms, and your preparation pays dividends.

Whenever young athletes begin to lose confidence, remind them that they are probably focusing too much on outcomes and results. It's a dead giveaway and quickly diagnosed with an easy prescription: control only what you can, do your best, and let results take care of themselves. Remind your athlete that he or she is prepared, has the skill set, and has enough talent to perform well. The key to confidence is expectations and focus. Don't focus on winning or losing but instead on how you're playing. Don't expect success or failure, but expect that you will execute the little things, perform to the best of your abilities, and have fun in the process.

The Success of Failure

We are all imperfect and will fail on occasions, but fear of failure is the greatest failure of all.

— John Wooden

Someone once said that 99 percent of success is failure. Walking the path of wisdom tells you that loss is gain, and to truly help your kids in athletics, you may want to teach the notion of failure as success.

If you look back on your life, you'll notice that your failures, setbacks, and mistakes were wonderful opportunities for you to grow and learn what it takes to forge ahead. For me, becoming computer literate was a process of correcting mistakes over and over until I mastered a particular process. Infants do this when they master the complex physical skill of walking. Failure is the teacher that helps us to learn well through pain, adversity, and loss.

I have several tips to offer that will help you to mindfully guide your athlete with this way of thinking. First, explain to your child that mistakes, errors, setbacks, and failures are nature's way of teaching us how to learn and improve. If your child is playing basketball, for instance, inform him or her that Michael Jordan is well known in basketball circles for always saying he became great because of his mistakes. Our failures in life help us to ultimately win and achieve.

Then I encourage you to be genuine, vulnerable, and transparent by sharing a personal situation in your life where failure actually helped you to go to new levels of achievement. I like to tell others that my bestselling book *Thinking Body, Dancing Mind*, which today appears in over ten languages and is still selling well after twenty-three years, was rejected from publication many times. Although I was discouraged every time a publisher declined my request, I saw each rejection as an opportunity to learn from the setback and to become a better writer. This book and that process actually launched my lifelong career.

I also suggest telling your young athletes that mistakes will always be part of life. You can reduce your fear and anxiety by embracing mistakes using this affirmation on a daily basis: "All my mistakes, errors, and failures are teachers that help me to get better and better." Then, to help children cope with a mistake when it first happens, ask them to be aware of and change their self-talk. It's normal for kids to get discouraged and say to themselves something like: "I suck. I'm not good enough. I don't deserve to play." However, encourage them to rephrase this self-talk, saying instead: "That mistake sucks. I can do better. Watch me, here I go." Focus criticism on the action, not the person; this places the word "sucks" where it belongs. Then reinforce the truth that "I can do better" and direct your child to express definitive action: "Watch me, here I go."

Whenever your child loses a game, has a setback, or makes a mistake, wait a day and then ask this thought-provoking question: "Why are you a better athlete now than you were before that loss or mistake?" By asking this question, you train your child to see the connection between the tough performance or loss and how it teaches us to improve every time. How important is this for the bigger game of life? Once this insightful question is answered, your child may be ready to respond to further analysis. Ask, "What went well?" There is always an upside to every performance, even if it's something simple like hustling, cheering teammates, or never giving up. Then, once your child sees that all is not lost, ask, "What needs work?" This is a more proactive approach than the all-too-familiar, reactive question: "What went wrong?" All of these questions open a kid's heart to possibility rather than inability. In this way, children learn that failure, although disappointing, is not as devastating as it seems.

Champions know that failure is a necessary prerequisite to success. Our kids will learn more from their setbacks than their successes. It is up to us as parents to consistently redirect our children toward this way of thinking. In the process, our children will experience less fear, anxiety, tightness, and tension, which, paradoxically, will contribute to a more relaxed, fluid, and successful performance next time. You will also feel like a good parent, more relaxed and calm as you learn to not internalize your child's external problems. Their issues are not your fault. You're a wonderful parent with pure intentions.

There is a wonderful Buddhist saying that addresses this

attitude of success coming from failure: "The arrow that hits the bull's eye is the result of a hundred misses." Your child improves in athletics and life through adversity and failure. Seeing failures as opportunities for success makes all setbacks more tolerable. Let them learn that tomorrow's another day, and it's all part of this extraordinary path of learning, growing mentally and emotionally, and developing the inner strength to develop one's full human capacity. Failure will always be disappointing, but it's never devastating. That one has not really failed when one fails is the ultimate paradox of life.

With your mindful guidance, your child will begin to understand that great athletes become great as they identify what they learn in defeat and turn that newfound knowledge into a gift for progressing to higher levels of play in the future. Having this positive approach to failure will help your kids to experience much success with sport, an activity that continually offers them the "opportunity" to fail.

When Fear Is Near

The other side of every fear is freedom.

— Alan Watts

F ear is a natural emotion for all of us, kids included. Fear indicates a need to be alert when there is danger. It is part of our survival instinct. Eventually, your child will experience fear related to performance in athletics.

To help athletes cope with fear, I distinguish between two types: rational fears and irrational fears. Some sports — such as cycling, skiing, football, gymnastics, and rock climbing — clearly involve the risk of physical injury. These sports can be dangerous, even at times life-threatening, and so an athlete may feel the onset of a rational fear that he or she could get hurt.

So-called irrational fears relate most often to a fear of failure or to an obsession with outcomes that cannot be controlled. Sometimes children simply become overwhelmed by the task in front of them or by the pressure of competition. In these situations, I remind athletes that FEAR is an acronym that stands for "false evidence appearing real."

However, whether a fear is rational or irrational, fighting against fear or trying to force it away creates a counterforce that makes you tense and anxious and interferes with your performance. How you cope with fear is as important as the fear itself and what it is about. Thus, as Alan Watts suggests in the quote above, our first task is to examine the fear, discern what it is about, and respond to it in the most appropriate way. If children feel afraid, ask why. Is it fear of physical injury? Do they feel unprepared? Do they have all the information they need? Are they out of their comfort zone? Help them assess the situation and then decide what to do. Are there actions or precautions you can take to emancipate yourself or your child from fear's grip, or is it an irrational fear with no evidence of danger? By identifying the source of fear, you help your child cope, identify a solution, and move forward, focusing on the possible actions you can take to avoid what is feared. As a parent of an athlete, you can help your child learn how to confront fear and make active choices.

Sometimes the fear your child experiences will be rational. For example, I was once cycling downhill on a wet, drizzly morning. The bike slid out from under me, causing multiple skin abrasions and sore bones and muscles. Afraid of having another accident, I avoided riding for weeks. The first time I was back on the bike, I descended a hill with a group of my training buddies, feeling like a beginner. I mentioned to someone that I was quite fearful of falling on sharp turns. His reply: "It's good that you have fear — you need to be cautious." He was right. I had not been cautious enough when I had fallen. My new fear helped me ride carefully and successfully in the downhill portion of the ride. I noticed that when I tried to fight my natural fear, I experienced a lot of tension in trying to force it away. This behavior would have eventually led to another accident. Instead, I needed to listen to my fear and act in ways that allowed me to feel safe enough to participate.

On the other hand, your child will sometimes feel irrational fears about losing or being afraid to perform. When this happens, help your child not look ahead or become focused on outcome. Divide the tasks of sports performance into small, manageable segments. Can you climb another two feet up? Can you ski just to that tree? Can you focus only on the next pitch? An Olympic marathoner once told me how, during one particular race, he became frightened that he'd blow his lead and possibly not even finish the race. Rather than dwell on that, however, he focused on running relaxed to the next mile while holding the lead. He did this for each of the last four miles, and to his surprise, he finished with energy to spare.

According to Taoism, approaching fear in this gradual way is the Chinese principle of *wu wei*, a way of working with fear by blending with its own force. *Wu wei* translates as "effortless action," whereby you accept the natural way (it's natural to have fear) and exert the least amount of energy possible when faced with such a situation. Don't fight fear or try to run away from it. Listen to its message, decide what the source is (whether it is rational or irrational), and then make proper adjustments. Because fear is a natural part of life, it doesn't go away. Fear can either paralyze us or present us with an opportunity to overcome obstacles, so long as we assess the risk and respond properly. Fear is a friend that you and your child can acknowledge and learn to embrace. In fact, these are lessons any of us can use and apply to our own life *when fear is near.*

Flow with the Plateau

Life is a series of natural and spontaneous changes. Don't resist them; that only brings sorrow. Let reality be reality. Let things flow naturally forward in whatever way they like.

— Lao Tzu

Chinese wisdom reminds us that the laws of nature are blueprints for *right action*. The idea is that we should notice what is happening, flow with it, and act accordingly. Everything happens for a good reason, even if we are unaware of what it all means. Birth, death, growth, maturity, and decline all happen according to nature's laws. Like the seasons, nature is cyclical. When you surrender to this cycle, let go, and give up the struggle to "make something happen," the answer or meaning is revealed.

This includes reaching plateaus in your child's athletic development. For young children in sport, and often for their parents as well, tolerating a lack of progress or forward movement is difficult to accept and understand, especially following much effort. The tendency is to want to push ahead even harder, to practice more, but this may only increase feelings of disappointment and frustration if little or no progress is made. Sometimes parents blame children for not trying hard enough, and sometimes parents blame themselves for not pushing hard enough. The truth is, plateaus happen; they are a natural part of the process of physical development and skill mastery.

If you and your child find yourselves in that nebulous, annoying place called a "plateau," know that it's nature's way of giving us an opportunity to truly master our present level of accomplishment. We need to achieve consistency with new skills before we move forward to the next level. In fact, most children must plateau before experiencing the next breakthrough. Most worthwhile learning takes place during the period of a plateau, and I encourage you to go with the flow when this happens. Plateaus are simply another stage along the path of mastery. Further, reassure your child athlete that it's perfectly fine to plateau, and with patience, persistence, and hard work, he or she will soon be rewarded again with measurable improvement. Of course, parents must also model this approach and be the change they want to see in their children. Are you patient and tolerant of your own plateaus? Our children are mirrors of everything we do, so we must be kind to ourselves and accept what life brings our way.

The plateau is a time when your child's mind and body catch up to a new level of performance. Why do we fight and battle with it? We are afraid, perhaps, that we will become complacent or stagnant and never go forward. Remind yourself of the truth: plateaus are a sacred space offering you and your child the chance to master what has recently been learned.

No need to get caught in society's pressure trap of achievement. Do not expect to go forward constantly. If you expect to have fun mastering each new level, expect to do well, and expect good to happen, you will, paradoxically, advance sooner. Let go of the need to achieve, and you will achieve. Go slower, arrive sooner!

Way of Mastery

The war is won before the battle begins.

— Sun Tzu, *The Art of War*

There is no way to mastery; mastery is the way. It is achieved through the daily practice of practice. When Sun Tzu states that the war is won before the battle begins, he means by your preparation prior to the event. I have learned from my experience with thousands of athletes that attention to detail through consistent, high-level, intentional practice positions us for extraordinary performance. I often tell my teams that when their practice becomes their toughest game, they will be difficult to beat. At the very best, having strong practice sessions enables athletes to achieve a lifestyle of mastery, doing their best to be their best on a consistent basis.

In Buddhist teaching, practice is the way of mastery. It's the eagerness to do everything necessary to be the absolute best you can be. The path of mastery may be a thousand miles, but it begins with a single, high-quality first step called diligent preparation. This focus on the initial step alone is considered success, and it's a principle that I teach for sports and for all of life.

The Chinese symbol for practice shows a young bird flapping its wings continually until it learns to fly. Your child can remember this metaphor when he or she wishes to "fly" in any arena of performance. Like nature's aviator, a child must repeat, over and over, the practice of a certain skill until the spirit takes flight, soaring to enormous heights.

I encourage my network of performers to practice each day as if they are preparing for an important recital or a national championship game; in other words, they should prepare with greater-than-usual focus, intention, and intensity. I invite them to prepare as if this were their last chance to prove their worth as performers. When they make this level of commitment, their performance is extraordinary. The great champions — athletes like Mia Hamm, Michael Jordan, Wayne Gretzky, and Peyton Manning — demonstrate the courage to prepare consistently in practice with game-time intensity.

You don't *become* a champion; you choose to *be* one right now, in practice. Cyclists know that mastery means time in the saddle, mile after mile. Trust that consistent, intentional preparation is, in itself, extraordinary behavior.

This principle of mastery is one that can be learned and therefore taught. Teach your children well through example, demonstrating how you personally embody this message in your work, hobbies, aspirations, and all aspects of life. When one of my children recently asked me how I learned to write, I told him that I have had much practice. I mentioned to him that I have adopted a lifestyle of consistent, daily attention to my goals through diligent practice. My kids witness it daily, and I make sure they see the connection with all I've accomplished because of my intentional work ethic. I recommend that you model this concept of mastery for your little stars as well.

Know, however, that you cannot "make" your child practice. Forcing or pushing a child to do something when he or she is not ready will backfire and be counterproductive. Parents can suggest, nudge, guide, and invite their child to entertain the idea of more practice, but nothing more. Also be aware that age and maturation are factors in a child's willingness to embody higher levels of dedication and commitment to a practice routine. A ten-year-old might reject an invitation to be more diligent with practice, but five years later the same child may easily embrace such a work ethic, independent of their parent's input.

The Significance of Influence

What you do makes a difference, and you have to decide what
kind of difference you want to make.

— Jane Goodall

I n this section, I wish to stress the relevance of your influence
on your children's behavior, performance, and lives in general.

First, your influence is never neutral. This is a crucial element
in the process of mindful mentoring and heartful guidance. Your
body language, tone of voice, gestures, and facial expressions communicate either distress or satisfaction. You walk into a room or a
gym, onto a field or a ball court, and you can either light up your
child or cast him or her in darkness. The more you are aware of
this power, the more influence you have in outcomes, results, and
behaviors in your child's world. As the German author Wolfgang
von Goethe once said, "I possess tremendous power to make life
miserable or joyous....I can humiliate or humor, hurt or heal."
How true are his words for all of us parents? And how about for

the coaches of young athletes? What I observe in my work is how unaware, how asleep, how mindless parents can be. Sometimes, parents approach their kid after a soccer game or other athletic event and "turn their lights out" by their overwhelmingly critical, negative commentary about their kid's bad performance or about the outcome, poor officiating, or lack of good play by others on the team.

The most challenging task for all of us as mindful parents is how to influence others in a positive way. It seems simple yet it isn't easy because it is often hard to stay focused in the moment. We can be full of our own thoughts and feelings and not be awake to our children's needs and feelings. When all we offer is critique, we not only fail to light a fire in a child's belly, we dowse any existing flames.

Since you always influence others, prior to engaging someone in a conversation, ask yourself: How can I communicate understanding, kindness, connectedness, and an overall sense of right action, goodwill, and positivity? Stay mindful prior to all engagements with others if your intention is to empower and inspire. How do others do this for you in your relationships? What behavior by others lights the fire in your belly? Just being aware of this more consistently can create the environment of openness, receptivity, and love, which is so important for positive change and growth in the sports lives of kids and their friends. Such awareness sets a positive, heart-directed tone to help move kids further along in sports and all of life.

Here is something I always do to stay mindful about the power of my influence in my team-building work with athletic programs across the nation. My desire is to be connected, empowering, and inspiring and to demonstrate my care for these athletes. When I enter the venue, I gather all the athletes into a huddle. While together, I say: "There are many beautiful, interesting places I can be. There are many fun things that I can be doing right now, but truthfully, there's no other place I'd rather be than here with you. I love being with you guys, doing our warrior work of the heart together." After I say this, I always feel the energy shift, as everyone's heart opens up wide to take in the awesome work we are about to begin.

What can really help you to spread your influence in a significant way? Remember to listen often, understand more fully by asking good questions, and follow up by validating these young stars when the opportunity comes. Let them know how much you love being with them and watching them play.

The Slump Bump

Slump? I ain't in no slump....I just ain't hitting.

— Yogi Berra

Where a *plateau* is reaching an acceptable level of performance and not moving forward, a *slump* is reaching that same level and moving backward. A slump is a speed bump that slows you down and sets you back temporarily. Like the plateau, a slump is a natural occurrence for all athletes at different stages in the development of their full human capacity.

The way out of a slump is simple, but like much in the life of young athletes, it's not easy. As a sports parent, you can help guide your kid through this frustrating period of self-doubt and lack of confidence.

The first step on the path of full recovery is not to fight the slump. The more your child fails to produce results, the more he or she will focus on getting results, which will create tension and anxiety and lead to more undesirable results. It becomes a vicious cycle.

Instead, ask your child to concentrate only on the little things, the essential ingredients so necessary for acceptable performance and beyond. A Buddhist proverb says, "From little streams come big rivers." When your child is in a batting slump, ask him or her not to focus on trying to get a hit. Instead, focus your child on his or her physical batting mechanics, keeping an eye on the ball at all times, taking a few deep breaths prior to entering the batter's box, and using this affirmation before each pitch: "I can hit, here I go, watch me." The same advice applies to any sport. As I mentioned earlier, basketball players can focus on boxing out, crashing the boards, diving for the loose ball, and playing tough defense.

In other words, focus on the process, on what can be controlled, and not on results. In this way, your child will become relaxed, calm, focused, and in control (of what can be controlled), and as a result, his or her confidence will return and performance will be enhanced. When you try to fight a slump — which is the method of choice for most athletes — you will create more pressure, tension, stress, and anxiety. Whenever you complicate a situation, performance goes south.

A sports parent recently brought her daughter, Kylie, to my office hoping I could help her break out of her slump. Kylie is the star forward on her high school soccer team, and seven games into the season, she had not scored one goal. I asked Kylie what she thought was happening. She told me that she felt pressure to score because college coaches were thinking of recruiting her after her amazing season the previous year. According to her, "If I don't score, I won't play in college." Kylie was (and still is) hoping to play at Stanford or Carolina, two of the top soccer schools in the nation. What pressure, right? I suggested to Kylie that she simply show up to compete by doing all the little essential things she could control, such as playing hard, working hard, practicing soccer drills, communicating constantly on the field with teammates, and enjoying being on the pitch. After two sessions together, Kylie let go of results and stats, focused on the controllables, and scored a hat trick (three goals in one game) in her very next game. She got over the slump bump and returned to her usual form.

During life's inevitable ups and downs, slumps are the lowest point in nature's perpetual pendulum swing. When your little star eventually lets go of trying to get out of the slump, things will slowly shift upward and normal performance will return. Forcing outcomes or results only delays the upward swing.

Remember, the genesis of a slump itself is often when players focus on results instead of executing all the little things, which is what led to success in the past. The mistake in a slump is trying hard to execute the big things. If you do, you tend to swing and miss.

Here is a final idea to share with your child: When the wind blows, the flexible bamboo tree yields and stays intact, while the rigid pine cracks and falls. Don't resist the force of the wind; relax. Suggest that your child take three deep breaths to relax before playing, and then visualize quietly how it feels when athletic performance is fluid, free, and flowing. Encourage your child to imagine what it's like to perform all the little things, letting go of outcomes. Only then will the good outcomes return.

Perfectly Imperfect

Perfection belongs to the gods; the most we can hope for is
excellence.

— Carl Jung

I n my work, one thing I notice is how many parents want their
kids to be perfect, and in turn, their children often strive to
fulfill those wishes. When this happens, parents become peren-
nially disappointed, and kids are never satisfied with their own
performance.

Over the last forty years, I have worked with many thousands
of young athletes between the ages of fifteen and twenty-two,
from high school to college, and I can honestly say that half of
these kids have suffered from what I call *perfection attention*, the
act of constantly being obsessed with being perfect. Having such
a lofty, unattainable goal positions them perfectly for failure. Yet
frustratingly, they keep measuring their self-worth as athletes
and people by outcomes and results, by winning and losing, by

achievements and failures. Parents play a huge role in this malady because they believe, usually unconsciously or unintentionally, that they are better parents if their kids are perfect. Intellectually, a parent may know that perfection is not possible, yet they feel there is no harm in trying. As a result, I often find myself working with kids who are terribly disappointed in themselves, awfully frustrated, and often angry about not measuring up.

I remember one parent who unintentionally held back his love if his kid's performance was lackluster. The athlete, wanting to be loved, felt the pressure to win, achieve, and be perfect. What I believe the father desired for his child was to experience the joy, fun, and excitement of being the best that we can be at whatever we attempt. But this message became convoluted and obscured as his love for his kid became conditional.

No one can achieve perfection, which is godlike, but the concept can still be useful as a beacon, as a goal or inspiration, that can keep us on track as we pursue excellence. This is an appropriate use of the standard of perfection. The concept names our intentions but not what we expect to achieve, nor is it how we measure our self-worth. This is what I call being *perfectly imperfect*.

I like to remind children that there are only two kinds of athletes: those who fail and those who will fail. By this I mean that we are all imperfect. Even the greatest of the great are imperfect. Professional baseball hitters are considered great if they get a hit a third of the time. Professional basketball players are considered excellent if they make half of their shots from three-point range. If soccer players, on average, make one goal for every five shots they attempt, they are celebrated. All athletes fail, make mistakes, commit errors, and lose. Those who are the best always mean to do their best, they strive to be the best they can be, and this puts them in a position for good things to happen…but not *perfect* things.

When youngsters believe that their efforts have to be perfect, they are set up for failure. As parents, we can help our children handle failure by being vulnerable ourselves and shattering any illusions our children have that we are perfect. We can share our imperfections and our imperfect journey in life with them. Of course, we always seek excellence, but no one always achieves it. I often remind my kids: "Hey, I'm not perfect. It's my intention to be good, but perfect is not me."

The notion and illusion that one can be perfect creates tension, stress, anxiety, and frustration. As a parent, notice the ways that you emphasize external achievement, care about others' opinions, fear failure, engage in criticism, dwell on negative outcomes, and disengage with an activity when you feel incapable. When you act this way, your kids get the unspoken message that they too must be perfect.

Affirm the following to your kids and yourself: "Performance can never be perfect, since perfection is an illusion, an unattainable waste of time and energy. Instead, I will strive for excellence by simply doing and being my best." This is being *perfectly imperfect*.

The Expectation Dilemma

Expect nothing, but be ready for anything.

— Samurai warrior saying

Regardless of your child's level of participation in sports, his or her performance will be greatly influenced by expectations. What I've seen from over a lifetime working with athletes is that expectations produce unwanted pressure and consistently result in limited and subpar performances. It doesn't matter if you expect good things or bad things. Expectations are all about the outcome and results, neither of which can be controlled, and this unproductive thinking therefore makes one tight, tense, and tentative, the holy trinity of self-destruction. Expectations come from many sources: they can be driven by coaches, especially those who need results to justify their existence; by overzealous parents seeking to inspire their kids (or perhaps vicariously live through them); by friends and teammates who only want to win;

and oftentimes by the child, who may be caught in the trap of measuring self-worth by external success.

Parents are in the perfect position to deflate this performance pressure by helping children understand the problems of having expectations. Whenever you talk with your child about his or her performance, be aware of any tension or unspoken expectations you may carry — since children always pick up on these silent messages, especially when they relate to your personal expectations for them.

Assuming athletes have prepared well, I encourage my athletes, coaches, and parents to embrace only three expectations: expect to do well (by demonstrating what you've practiced and learned), expect good things to happen (such as executing a game plan or doing things correctly), and expect to have fun (by enjoying the process, being with your friends, and learning the game). If preparation is lacking, adjust these expectations accordingly. You can always still have fun by enjoying playing and the learning process, but if you are still mastering basic skills, you may not perform well. When children embody these types of expectations, taking them into their nervous systems, they relax, become calm, remain focused, and play their best. These are *process* expectations as opposed to outcome expectations. While this may seem counterintuitive, I have had remarkable success with this approach. It completely shifts one's perspective and enhances all performance. According to the wisdom of the *Tao Te Ching*:

> With expectation, one will always perceive the limitations.
> Evolved individuals act without expectation and succeed.

Do you know what makes the difference between a good performance and a bad one (or a good day and a bad day)? It's very simple: good performances more often happen when you have no expectations, let your activity unfold, and trust things to work out. You can then relax and focus on the series of actions you need to carry out, which are the little things you can control. Bad performances, on the other hand, happen when you try to control the end result and have high expectations. As I mentioned before, trying to control what you can't — the finished product — causes anxiety and tension. This may be the biggest issue facing youngsters around sports performance.

The Chinese symbols for *expectation* show the enjoyment of someone watching the rising and setting of the moon in its natural arc across the sky. In my way of thinking, if your child can flow with nature's organic process and enjoy the work fully in the moment, he or she will truly be fulfilled and will feel successful in sport and life.

"But I want to win," a child athlete may say. Tell him or her, "You will win *if you refuse to expect to win*." This is a very Zen idea; it is a paradox, but it is also true. If you practice nonattachment to results, your body will be less tight, tense, and stressed, and it will become more relaxed and calm, which leads to playing at a higher level, which increases the prospects of actually winning. If you let go of the need to win, you will be victorious. Maybe not in the game, but in your effort to do well, which is another way of defining what winning is all about.

Consider writing the following on an index card and reading it to your child every day:

I focus on my practice, my preparation, and the process of my performance plan; when I do, I can expect the best to happen, whatever it may be.

The Power of Thought

We are shaped by our thoughts. We become what we think.

— Buddha

When I am working with athletes, I encourage them to be aware of their thoughts. These are often expressed in the words we use regularly when we talk to ourselves. These expressions impact our performance. In fact, I believe that the single most important element for success in life is the words we use to express our thoughts. Choosing strong positive words strengthens us and closes the gap between where we are and what's ultimately possible. Focusing on negative words and thoughts will weaken us. Thoughts are the core of our mental and emotional strength. They have a power of their own, and they determine the direction you will go in sports and life. If you'd like to do something, but you think you can't, you will never be able to do it. Your words and thoughts must align with your intentions to reach what you desire. I have interspersed affirmations throughout this book for this reason. I hope you will use them to influence the way you think and, thereby, perform.

There's an old story I like to tell about a little boy who says to his dad, "I am having a bad day today, but yesterday was great. Why is that, Dad?" His dad replies, "Son, there are two wolves inside all of us, a good wolf and a bad wolf, and they are always fighting. The bad wolf says that you are weak, slow, not good enough, can't do it, and never will be happy. The good wolf, fighting back, says that you are strong, fast, good enough, can do it, and will be happy for a long time." The boy asks the dad, "Who will win?" The dad replies, "The one who wins is the one you feed."

I think this is a good story to share with child athletes, and if it speaks to you, consider sharing it with yours. It vividly dramatizes how our inner thoughts and words often determine our actions and performance. Athletes at all levels of play are fully aware of this concept, and any child can benefit from it, in sports or not.

Here is another way to illustrate the power of thoughts with your child. As an experiment, ask your kid to hold one arm straight out to the side and keep it up while saying over and over, "I can do it, I am strong." As he or she does, you gently and slowly apply pressure to push the arm down. Then try it again: with the same arm extended, have your child say, "I can't do it, I'm too weak," as you again gently and slowly push down. Notice the difference in arm strength when the different phrases are recited. This exercise embodies the message that the body follows our thoughts. Negative words create self-doubt, tension, and tightness, and our arms respond accordingly. Positive thoughts keep the blood flowing and allow the muscles to do their job.

Another useful strategy is to teach your child to use affirmations: to repeat positive, present-tense, short statements that define the direction we want to go or how we want to be. In addition to those provided elsewhere in the book, some simple affirmations for kids could be: *I do my best to play my best*; or *I am a talented, strong, competitive athlete*; or *I play well and expect good things to happen*. For very young kids, parents might consider reciting positive affirmations *to* their child, rather than asking the child to say them. Parents could regularly tell their children: *you are healthy and strong*; or *you play quite well*; or *it's fun to watch you play*. Basically, parents can model the behavior they wish for children to learn. Then, if you hear your child using a negative affirmation — such as, "I stink, I can't do this" — suggest changing it so that it isn't a self-criticism. Coach your child to say, "Yeah, that was awful, but I can do better, watch me."

As Bob Marley suggested, we all must work to emancipate ourselves from mental slavery because no one but us can alter our minds.

Worthy Opponent

For self-realization, a rebel demands a strong authority, a worthy opponent.

— Mary McCarthy

The Chinese philosophy of Taoism emphasizes the importance of mutual dependence and oneness with others. Everyone has a mutual need to be respected, to be treasured for what we bring to the world. Separation is an illusion. The needs of others are the same as ours. How appropriate are these thoughts when we face an opponent in sport or life?

Traditionally, an opponent in sport is considered an enemy, someone to be overcome and defeated by whatever methods possible. Yet Chinese wisdom reminds us to embrace our opponent or our competition. Interestingly enough, the word *competition* comes from a Latin root meaning "to seek together." Here is a deeper, more mindful way to know one's opponent as a partner in a relationship of cooperation; each offers the best they have to help bring out the best in the other. Personally, I feel great satisfaction when I compete against an opponent who challenges me to be the best I can be. A worthy opponent can help us discover our greatness.

This approach can be very helpful for child athletes; when we seek together the mutual benefits of intense competition, we embrace competition as a goal in itself. This values process over results. In Zen thought, we each seek to be a "worthy opponent." We offer our best possible performance so that other competitors are forced to dig deep and respond with their best. When this happens, all involved can reach levels of play never imagined possible.

In other words, I suggest that you, as a sports parent, help your young athlete to love the opponent. How different is this concept? Why do so many of us waste emotional, physical, and mental energy hating those we compete against? This "despising the enemy" approach is counterproductive to playing well. Anger, hate, and force may inspire intense effort in the short term, but in the long run, these feelings diminish our concentration and dilute our energy and motivation.

I encourage you to teach your child this softer yet stronger way to compete. Regard athletic competitors as partners who help to bring out our best on any given day. Your child can still play hard, battle, and go all out, but the goal changes. Instead of striving to defeat the opponent, we seek to inspire the best performance in one another, and through our fierce efforts, we each become "worthy opponents." The better one plays, the better the other will play. This is a new, healthier, more relaxed, and more productive way to compete, as partners seeking everyone's personal best performance.

Beyond Limitations

Whether you think you can or think you can't, you are right.

— Henry Ford

D id you know that the bumble bee shouldn't be able to fly? *Really?* you ask. Well, according to several researchers, it's too fat, too heavy, too slow, and its wings are not wide enough for it to fly. It doesn't seem to possess any of the essential traits so necessary for successful flight. Yet these "aviators," with a life span of only seven weeks, fly over 37,400 miles in their lifetime. Doing the math, that's 763 miles a day at thirty-one miles per hour, flying to gather a total of only one-twelfth of a teaspoon of honey from all that work during its entire existence. I can't even drive a car that far in a single day without getting exhausted.

Then there is the story about the ninety-three-year-old man who hikes twenty-five to thirty miles a day. When asked how he could achieve such a feat, he replied, "No one ever told me I couldn't do it."

Stories like these must be told to our athletic children, whose nervous systems are marinated in the disabilities of life rather than its possibilities. Through the media, we are bombarded daily by negative comments and messages, so it's no wonder we assume "I can't" before we test the waters of what is possible. Thinking "I can" motivates me to do what needs to be done in order to progress. If I say, "No, it can't be done," I'll decide not to do the work because, of course, why bother if I won't succeed anyway? Besides, I never want to prove myself wrong.

A famous illustration of the power of belief is Roger Bannister, who in 1954 became the first person to run a mile in under four minutes. This story is worth retelling to our kids, who often assume they know their limits and so fail to use their gifts to perform at higher levels. Prior to Bannister's run, over fifty reputable medical journals throughout the world claimed that such speed by a human was not only impossible, but unthinkable. Everyone accepted that four minutes was a physical barrier. Once Bannister transcended that limit, the sub-four-minute mile immediately became commonplace. Over the next year and a half, over forty-five athletes matched Bannister's time. Few believe that all those runners magically became faster all at once. The more likely explanation is that once this supposed barrier was broken, people could believe in new possibilities. This limit was an illusion — a figment of the imagination, a perception of the mind.

John Lilly, a researcher and neuroscientist, once said, "Beliefs are limits to be examined and transcended." When we believe that we can accomplish a certain task, we probably can and will;

when we believe we can't, we will probably prove ourselves correct. Have you ever not accomplished something that you knew you could do and that you wanted to accomplish? Have you ever had preconceived ideas about your own limitations, only to go beyond them and realize that you are capable of so much more than you once imagined?

Researcher Dr. Georgi Lozanov has said, "We are conditioned to believe that we can only learn so much so fast, that we are bound to be sick, that there are certain rigid limits to what we can do and achieve, and we are bombarded constantly with limiting suggestions....Belief in limits creates limited people....Both history and experimental data show that humans possess vastly larger capabilities than those they now use."

According to author Dr. Jean Houston, "We are just beginning to discover the virtually unlimited capacity of the mind." From my experiences, I believe we cannot come close to imagining our greatest potential. I can see no limits (although ultimately we may reach some). If you question this statement, I ask you to truly ask yourself: Have I pushed out far enough to find out if the limits I believe in truly exist? There always seems to be more that we can be or do.

I encourage you and your child to stay open and receptive to possibility, especially in sports, but also in life. Help your child, as John Lilly suggests, to examine beliefs and go beyond them. Be proactive when you hear your child say, "I can't do that" or "I'm not good enough." As I've suggested, encourage them to change their self-talk and practice affirmations like "I can do it, I am strong." Practice mindful awareness of the messages we send ourselves. Are they messages of limitations or of possibilities?

In his classic book *Zen Mind, Beginner's Mind*, Shunryu Suzuki writes: "In the beginner's mind there are many possibilities; in the expert's mind there are a few." All of us, not only children, should practice beginner's mind. Refuse to allow preconceived biases to prevent you from realizing your full human capacity.

Selfless Caring

Nothing can give you greater joy than doing something for another.

— John Wooden

My Brooklyn upbringing taught me to put myself first and avoid being last at all costs. Today, I notice that when I act without self-interest, my interests paradoxically become fulfilled.

Even in Christian mysticism, the truly selfless, humble people are recognized as worthy. Most holy books agree with this sacred concept of selflessness.

I often say that my work is not a job, it's a calling; I work not to make money but to make a difference. When I work in that heart space, the money comes and I make a good living. To me, I am a servant in life; I seek to give without getting. Yet the more I give, the more I seem to get. Life is funny that way. You may believe this or have noticed this, too, yet how often do we forget that the sole reason for our existence is to serve others? Service is our highest calling, and guess who taught me this. Each of my kids, in more ways than I care to remember. While they truly remain my Zen masters, they are no longer in residence. They come back, but they are now adults who have moved on and are making their own way. I am grateful to them for teaching me to grow up and to be their servant. Well, not really...but I am happy they taught me the gift of giving.

I love the ancient Eastern story about how heaven and hell are exactly alike. Each is an enormous banquet with an abundance of delectable dishes placed on tables in one big room divided by a curtain. All who participate are given chopsticks five feet long. In hell, each person struggles and suffers trying to feed him- or herself, but everyone is unsuccessful and remains unfulfilled. In heaven, everyone selflessly picks up food and feeds the person across the table.

Selflessness is an active process of devotion to others' welfare. Selflessness is personal power. Taoists call it *tz'u*, which means caring selflessly. As sports parents, when we model this trait on a daily basis, we teach it to our children. We can ask our child athlete, how can you give to your team today at practice? Most kids show up to get...whether that's more playing time, more at bats, more recognition, or more fun. Rarely does a coach hear these magic words: Hey coach, what can I do for you today? Before a game or event, we can ask our children: How can you best contribute to your team today, before, during, and after the game?

Many kids (and parents) these days worry about playing time. The only thing that "counts" is the game, and practice is considered a waste if those game-time minutes are not enough.

This is another example of focusing on results, not process. If this includes you or your child, consider the following story. For fifteen years, basketball athlete Andre Iguodala of the Golden State Warriors was a starter, and often an all-star, on every team on which he ever played. Then in the 2014–15 season, he was asked by his coach, Steve Kerr, to take a nonstarting role. Kerr believed it would help the team best if André came into the game off the bench, bringing new, fresh energy to the team when it needed it most. Andre accepted this unfamiliar change, and his more limited role, all season. Ultimately, however, the Warriors reached the NBA finals that season, playing against the Cleveland Cavaliers. The Warriors were down two games to one, and Steve Kerr felt his team needed some new energy, so he asked Andre to start in the fourth game. Andre did and played like a man possessed; the Warriors went on to win the NBA championship, and Andre was awarded the MVP of the finals. This amazing tale of selflessness and giving should be a lesson remembered by all aspiring athletes and their parents.

As a parent, model selflessness and find personal fulfillment in giving. Ask "How can I help?" when someone seems in need, and then don't be surprised when your child begins to do the same.

Here is an affirmation about selflessness to recite often:

To create more joy for myself and others, I remind myself and my child, when we give, we get back a hundredfold. This is nature's basic law of selflessness and reciprocity.

PART THREE

Navigating Uncharted Waters

Lessons for Personal
and Athletic Awareness

Finding Your Own Purpose

If you look to your children to provide meaning
for your life, your life will be meaningless.
Your children were not born to complete your life.
They were born to complete their own.

— William Martin, *The Parent's Tao Te Ching*

I love the way Bill Martin translates this passage from the *Tao Te Ching*, the Chinese spiritual text describing the natural way of power. It sounds like he has all of us sports parents in mind. For me, I remember the exact moment of personal awakening when I realized I was seeing my third son, Brennan, as an extension of myself…a mini-me, actually. I unintentionally or subconsciously was living my life through his sport, distance running. Early on in Brennan's career, before I knew better, I found myself running the last mile of a three-mile cross-country race by his side, coaching and cheering him on, until the meet director intervened and told me to stop. What I was doing was illegal, and the director could have disqualified Brennan from the race, which, fortunately, he did not do. This moment was extremely embarrassing to both my son and me. Brennan was a talented highschool runner who eventually received a scholarship to the University of Colorado, something I had missed out on as a young athlete. At that time, I was looking for athletic meaning in my life, and Brennan's career offered me a chance to redo or relive what I had hoped I could be: a champion runner in college. As I write this story, I am still embarrassed by my behavior, but I am happy I learned my lesson. It changed my life. Of course, part of me wanted to win through my son, but mostly, my intention was to help him experience success and feel proud of himself.

When we look around today, we see countless parents overly invested in their children's success. It's normal to care and want to help. As parents, we *are* invested, but we all must learn to be awake and pay attention so as not to interfere with our children. As I learned firsthand, it is easy to be a well-intentioned sports parent and still overdo it, to get caught in the trap of wanting our child to "catch the next train" to Stanford or any other prestigious learning institution.

We need to remember that sports are their thing, not ours. Kids don't play sports for Mom or Dad. They play to have fun, and most kids care little or nothing about winning. Naturally, they want to be successful and feel competent, and they want their parents to love them and watch them play. Overzealous parents who go "over the top" interfere with these goals. For instance, a sports mom recently told me the following story. Her nine-year-old son came home from his baseball game, and she asked him, "How was your game?" The boy thought for a moment, then replied: "It was great. We lost, but we really had the most fun." Because the boy's team had the most fun, they won, not on the scoreboard, but in their hearts, in the world of play. Parents must remember it's their game and to let children play and enjoy sports for their own reasons.

This is why it's important for parents to find their own purpose. When parents rely on their children for meaning, it sends the wrong message. When parents seek purpose or validation in their children's sports, children come to feel as though parental love is based on their performance. For the child, it's a simple equation: win and gain your parents' love and acceptance. Lose and be criticized or shunned. Most parents don't mean to act this way, but subtle reactions may send this message. Then again, sometimes this message is overt.

A collegiate athlete recently told me how her father wasn't showing up to her games because she wasn't playing well. He told her, "It's not fun watching you play these days, so why should I come?" He was being honest, but also quite insensitive and harsh. Needless to say, his daughter was terribly distraught by his callous remarks and behavior. Later, I met with the father, and from our conversation, I felt he had a rather low sense of self. He wanted his daughter to be a winner in part because it helped him feel better about himself. The father was living vicariously through his daughter. When she played well, it masked his own shortcomings; when she did not, he felt exposed as a loser. In fact, I have found that this problem of self-involved sports parenting seems to be nearly universal, at least to varying degrees. To change such behaviors, we must become mindful, aware, and awake. When we do, we make a huge difference in the lives of our kids.

As I say, sports parenting is difficult, yet it provides an opportunity for wonderful, authentic inner growth for all. My life

partner and wife, Jan, and I have learned our lessons. We listen
to our kids and encourage them to follow their hearts, not ours.
I feel fortunate that life has been good to my family, but it hasn't
come easy. Good sports parenting never ends. It is a constant
vigil, one of learning that we must allow our children to complete
their own lives, not ours.

I remain a happy parent after all my difficult experiences because my kids dare to follow their inner voice, what their hearts
tell them to do, and they seem well-adjusted and to be having fun
seeking fulfilling lives and discovering their true selves.

> To dare is to lose one's footing momentarily.
> Not to dare is to lose oneself.
>
> — Søren Kierkegaard

Be a Good Waiter

It is wise to abide by unnecessary intervention, avoiding entering others' process at all times. Be unobtrusive and not overbearing.

— Chinese wisdom

Wise, mindful sports parents are like good waiters. They are always within reach, yet they rarely intervene unnecessarily, refusing to constantly intrude. We have all experienced untrained and unconscious, obtrusive waiters: They show up while you have a mouthful of food and ask, "How is your dinner?" They visit the table a thousand times to fill the water glass and confirm that everything's all right, thoughtlessly interrupting the intimate conversation you and your partner are having. I waited tables in my younger years and quickly learned to watch and listen for the signals for assistance before I entered that special space of the customer.

Like a good waiter, practice watching from the wings of your child's space, and let them self-govern without your constant intervention. We must trust their process. Though we set the table, our children know, or will learn, how to feed themselves. Through sports, they learn how they move, how they think, what they need, how much, and when. If we allow our children to learn for themselves, they will be much happier, and they will trust us more in turn. Too often we micromanage our sports kids, perhaps out of insecurity or a fear of losing control. Paradoxically, if we want more control, we need to step back and let go of control. We won't lose our children if we let them find their own way. It's when we hold on tightly that our children feel the need to escape.

This is easy to say, but it hasn't come easy to me. Even now, I must practice staying in the wings of my kids' lives, even though they are in their twenties and early thirties. As they go forward with their personal and work-related adventures, I still make mistakes, thinking that "Father knows best." When, like a bad waiter, I interrupt too much, they tell me, "Chill out, Dad, we can handle this."

From the perspective of our sports kids, parents should be seen but not heard…unless, of course, they want to be driven to the mall. Children love knowing their parents are there, but they would rather not have parents step in and solve every problem, tell them how to do something, or make their decisions for them. They prefer to have autonomy until they need specific help. When we are needed, our children let us know — not always directly, but if we watch and listen, we'll see when they freak out over something and need our reassurance and guidance. What is required of us is to simply love our children and let them know we will be there whenever they need us. Isn't that what a good waiter does?

Do less, step aside, and free yourself from irrelevant mental clutter. Do nothing and everything will happen as it is supposed to. Soft is strong in these situations.

Walk a Mile in Their Cleats

Wise leaders immerse with others, refusing to act judgmentally.
In this way, they have open ears, hearts, and minds, more able to
understand the needs of others.

— Chinese wisdom

Listening to your athletic child helps to demonstrate respect,
caring, love, and trust. It makes your child feel valued and
worthwhile, which are necessary feelings if you want them to perform at their best. Be sure to avoid blame, lecturing, or criticism.
Listening on a deeper, conscious level helps a child to exhibit loyalty and compliance. The truth is, this advice doesn't just apply to
sports parenting but to all relationships.

I regretfully remember both of my parents uttering those unconsciously demeaning words: "Children should be seen and not
heard." Translated, this meant that if I had something to share
about the race I had run that day, it was not worth listening to.
Worse, this often made me feel that I was not worth listening
to. I felt unsafe in this environment, which stifled my growth,

expansion, and participation in all sports. I was discounted by my parents, and their cold words of disrespect often extinguished my fire for athletics. In fact, I dropped out of sports in high school, and I did not return until many years later. Perhaps I experienced an extreme case of parental callousness, but it taught me a vital lesson: to know our children, and earn their respect, we must "walk a mile in their cleats." We must listen to them and "immerse" ourselves in their lives and perspective. To gain a good sense about their lives and needs, we must make conscious efforts to listen more carefully and more often.

This is really very easy. Most of the time, we only need to ask about their experiences, concerns, and suggestions. By so doing, we contribute to their self-esteem and create an environment that is warm, caring, and cooperative, one where learning, growth, and excellence can thrive.

A fifteen-year-old pro tennis client of mine beautifully, if sadly, demonstrated what happens when parents refuse to listen to their young athletes. On the verge of burnout, she repeatedly told her dad, "I don't want to practice this anymore." He refused to hear her cry for help and forced her to play, insisting that she always stay prepared for the next tournament. Over time, and after several sessions together with me, she told me that she wanted to drop out of the pro tour, and she soon did. Later, she could never regain her form and ranking. Her father now admits that he made a mistake; he should have listened to his daughter and let her take a break when she needed one. Unfortunately, now it's too late for her pro career.

To be a good sports parent, there are two basic requirements: a lot of driving and a lot of listening. Everything falls into place when both are achieved. Listening to children sends a strong message of caring, and it acknowledges the importance of their participation in sports. The greatest impact on our children's development in sports, and all of life, is not from what we say but what we hear when we listen with love and intention.

Inspire through Consistency

Consistency ensures self-reliance and inspires self-direction. Parent and guide your child with love and oneness. Follow nature's course, the Tao, with full-heartedness.

— Chinese wisdom

As a sports parent, remember that inconsistent, unpredictable behavior patterns with your little stars are unsettling and can erode the confidence and trust so essential for a productive and harmonious relationship. Such chaos certainly is reflected in the inconsistent, mercurial sports performances of children.

Parents are most effective and influential when their actions are consistent and comfortably familiar. Ask yourself: How would I feel in an environment where I always had to walk on eggshells, in which inconsistency and unpredictability were the norm? Parents create love, order, safety, and comfort when they are consistent; they create disorder and chaos when they are not. Children already live with so much inconsistent behavior in their lives. To balance this, get in touch with the voice of your heart and transmit what works for you to others in your environment. Try to be consistent in your approaches and ways of being, and avoid erratic behavior that would create insecurity, tension, and fear in your kids. Be accountable and dependable with the variations of the patterns of sports life, and be clear with your core intentions to instill trust and mutual ease and comfort with your child. For example, try to behave consistently whether talking with the coach, picking your kids up after practice, volunteering as a team parent or in any other situation where your presence and attention is required. This way of being will inspire and empower your youngster and develop a long-lasting trusting relationship.

Less Control, More Control

There's an ancient story about a farmer who wanted to have more control over his cows. Rather than move the fences closer and pull the cows in, the farmer moved the fences farther out and only then, given more space to roam, did the cows have no desire to run away.

So it is with our athletic kids. When it comes to control, less is paradoxically more. Mindful parents refuse to micromanage and interfere with the process and progress of their athletic kids. Some parents, I notice, are overly visible, overzealous, and overbearing at games and even at some practices. These self-absorbed parents seem to believe they are not doing their job unless they are always checking up on their kid's progress, making suggestions to the coach, telling the athlete how to perform, and basically attempting to control every facet of the sports journey. I believe that by acting this way parents may be indicating their own levels of personal insecurity, and their actions condition their child athlete to feel the same way.

Parents who try to control their children can keep their children from developing self-reliance, vision, creativity, and courage. To me, an important role of youth athletics is to provide safe environments for young people to test their wings — to try and fail, over and over, until they succeed. Child athletes who come to depend on a parent's presence don't go through this process and learn its lessons. In this way, parents who control less help their children to realize their full potential for themselves.

The Chinese symbol for *control* emphasizes the way of letting go, which is allowing our kids to grow through loving kindness and guidance. As the Buddha says, when teachers give students the space to grow and explore, students discover their greatness.

As I suggest elsewhere, watch and listen to your child athlete, but don't step in to help unless they ask or you see things get out of control. Let children discover their ability to resolve problems as they arise.

A basic rule of thumb under most circumstances is to exert less control, let children flow, let children fly, let children have fun, and most of all, *let them play*.

The Delicateness of Readiness

When the student is ready, the teacher appears.

— Chinese wisdom

I often hear from coaches and parents about children who are not playing up to their potential. These particular kids seem unmotivated and unwilling to do the work. This issue gets raised about kids of every age, from six to sixteen. What, parents and coaches ask me, can they do to inspire talented kids to work hard?

What I've learned is that no amount of pushing or forcing will help. Each child matures at his or her own pace, and if a child is not ready, parents and coaches can't make them ready. Naturally, parents are concerned that their kids may miss an opportunity in this moment to advance and succeed. What I tell them is that there will always be another moment, and the teacher will be there when the child is ready.

The truth is, our kids are always ready...for something. It just may not be for sports or for what we think is important. We must remember that even as adults we are not always ready for certain "opportunities." Life continually presents us with options we decline. For example, just because we reach retirement age, that doesn't mean we are ready to retire. Some will be, some won't be, and others will probably never stop working. Why should our kids be any different when it comes to sports? We will experience a lot less frustration and confusion if we approach our children's motivation and maturation with patience, kindness, and understanding.

Our work as sports parents is not to make our kids do certain things or pursue athletic careers. Our work is to provide safe, uncritical environments where our child athletes feel comfortable playing sports, competing, and testing themselves. This takes encouragement, gentle guidance, and unfading patience. This is the only way I know to accelerate the process of getting kids to become ready for a serious sports commitment. Tentative, uncertain, or complacent kids, like adults, need much love.

As with so many issues, sports parents need to guard against the trap of taking a child's lack of drive or indifferent performance personally. Sometimes we become disappointed, frustrated, annoyed, confused, perplexed, and baffled by what seems to be an unwillingness in children to try or to give it their all, as if they are afraid to go the distance. We may blame ourselves and wonder why we can't motivate our kids the way other children seem to be motivated.

I truly believe that no one can motivate another person; no coach, no parent, and no teacher can get kids to do what they are not ready to do. All motivation comes from within. The only thing parents can do is provide a calm, relaxed, nurturing environment where these young warriors will feel more empowered and inspired to step forward and join the journey, which will always be at their own level and in their own way. Kids progress according to their own internal clock, and they will only move forward when they want to. This issue always reminds me of the old joke: How many psychologists does it take to change a lightbulb? Only one, but the bulb must want to change.

My kids are now young adults, and they continue discovering new ways to be in the world that make sense to them. Recently, one of my sons asked me, "Dad, have you ever tried meditating before the day begins?" In actuality, I've been meditating for years, and ten years ago I tried to introduce my kids to the practice of daily meditation. Oh well! I guess my timing was off.

Your work as a good sports parent is to add fuel to your kid's pilot light. When you do this, they eventually open their hearts to your teachings about how to advance and improve. When they give you permission to enter their hearts, your best work will be done, and they will believe in you and believe that they can be something other than ordinary.

To facilitate creating this safe environment, we must make it okay for kids to experience failure, setbacks, and mistakes. Remind your children of this, pointing out how failures are our teachers. Listen to your kid's concerns, offer your help, then retreat to the sidelines and wait for them to approach you for your advice. Keep trying, don't give up, and never take it personally. Every kid has a different learning curve.

Finally, remember that what you think is best for your child may not be what they desire. If they want to travel a different path, let them follow their own hearts and discover what turns them on, what they feel passion for, both in sports and in life. Treat opportunities like buses. When one stops, read the destination sign, and invite your children to climb aboard; no need to shove them on. There is always another bus coming, one that could be a better option that is going to a more attractive place. You want your little athletes to be happy, to have fun, and to play for all the right reasons. It will make your lives together happier and a lot less stressful.

Magical Victory Tour

Several years ago, I wrote a story about my experience while running with deer in the Big Sur hills along the California coast. I've told this story to thousands of athletes because it continues to serve as the perfect metaphor for excelling in sports and life. I call it my "magical victory tour" with the deer. I want to share this real-life tale with you now, so you will understand what I mean when I say that performance is not about the results but about the process. True victory is in the journey, not the destination, as the late, great tennis star Arthur Ashe once proclaimed. Here is that story, and I encourage you to share it with your children:

> Someone once claimed, "Sports are boring. How can any-
> one do this every day?" There is no way that one could

respond to this opinion or answer this question. One simply must experience the ecstasy and joy, the carefree lightness, the tranquil calm and vulnerability that such movement and play create. For me, "dancing" up a mountain pricks my senses and creates an opportunity to play like a child. I try not to ponder the questions too long: Will I reach the top? Will it hurt? I focus instead on my physical experiences with the deer people, those four-legged beings who jolt me back to the primeval as they glide up the hillside doing their effortless dance over each succeeding ridge. I simply try to chase after them, hoping they will play with me. Sometimes I win; sometimes I don't.

On one occasion, I was running after a small herd when a young buck came to a quick stop and began to charge toward me. Initially frightened by this aggressive move, I began to realize it was all in play; the deer were inviting me to tour the land with them. I chose to do so as we floated together across the wide majestic mountain meadows. I was one of them; I was a deer. I became a good animal, at one with nature, in touch with a greater sense of self, feeling the magic of being in the moment and totally letting go.

As I continued my tour across more ridges, I noticed hovering above a familiar-looking hawk who probably thought I was crazy. I knew it was a red tail by the way the late afternoon light reflected through its scarlet feathers as it glided effortlessly on an updraft. I continued to dance and flow through the steep canyons and ravines, smelling the medicinal scents given off by huge groves of eucalyptus trees. I could hear the muffled sound of thunder in the distance. The sky to the west was a brilliant blue changing to orange and deep red. As it twisted through the atmosphere, the light from the sun created an intense clarity with all things. As the sun set, the Steller's jays warned me that night was approaching. The moon in all its brilliance bathed the mountain in silver sheen.

Upon another ridge at the height of dusk, I spotted a rather suspicious bobcat, a peaceful, motionless king snake, and a new playful herd of deer. I wondered where they were all going — where they came from. I continued with the deer on a gallop up the next hill only to realize at that moment that I was at the very peak in almost total darkness. I had achieved my goal without trying to achieve it.

Obviously, reaching the top of anything in life is considered the pinnacle of success. This time, however, victory for me was the joy, exhilaration, harmony, and flow I experienced in the process of getting to that peak. I am a human being, not a human doing. This physical experience forced me to, as Ram Dass teaches, "be here now."

Such a "magical victory tour" is available to all of us, especially our children, whether dancing with the deer or participating in sports. Pure play is a sacred mental space of being in a special zone, with no mind, no thought beyond play. It is a path of least resistance, where the goal is not victory on the scoreboard but playfulness itself. Victory is experiencing joy; fun is true success. After all, there really is no purpose in sport other than to sustain this joy in effortless fashion as one becomes aligned with the dance of sports and life. Empower your child with this message . . . and yourself as well.

The Trying Tryout

Rejection doesn't mean you're not good enough; it means the other person failed to notice what you have to offer.

— Mark Amend

Not making the team...ouch! That hurts. Every fall is a "trying time" in the lives of sports parents. While rejection is a challenging experience, it is never (or rarely) as bad as it seems. Everyone experiences rejection at some point, and what we do in response is what determines our future achievements. I have experienced rejection in sports, in publishing, and in job applications. Each time, I felt disappointment and frustration, but I used those outcomes to fuel my resolve, determination, and persistence to succeed. Like Michael Jordan — who was once cut from his high school basketball team and who often cited the inspiration he drew from his failures — I can safely say that these trying times were essential for all my later success.

This isn't much comfort in the moment. Tryouts are difficult, scary times for kids and parents alike. If your child doesn't make the team, he or she will often feel some combination of disappointment, hurt, depression, anger, and fear. Acknowledge and accept these emotions, and allow your child to experience and mourn this loss. Help them process their feelings around this "death." Parents are in the best position to nurture and guide their children through these turbulent waters, which many children are experiencing for the first time.

Adults know that rejection stings, it hurts, but they also know the hurt doesn't last. The good news is that this experience is short-lived. It will pass, especially as kids move on and focus on "what's next." Parents can help children gain this perspective. Encourage your child to see that rejection is a pervasive experience in all aspects of life. It is ubiquitous and unavoidable, and it affects everyone from time to time.

Since how children manage this process is often directly related to how their parents react, you need to be mindful of your own emotional response and attitude. For instance, when parents get angry and confront coaches over their decisions, parents inflame and add drama to an already-emotional situation for the child. This response can be well-intentioned, but it's important to take a deep breath, count to ten, and be mindful of your child's feelings and response. After all, a coach is not likely to change his or her decision, and no child wants to make a team because of a parent. Rather, focus on helping your child move on, trusting that he or she will. Explore other options for that sport, or perhaps for getting involved in other sports or activities. Focus on the next opportunity, on the next bus your child might take, so that getting cut and a sense of failure do not infiltrate other segments of your child's life.

What else can you do when your child gets cut? My dear friend and trusted colleague Dr. Alan Goldberg has had much experience dealing with this issue. He's helped many to navigate the tenuous times of a trying tryout. I love his ideas, and I offer you his advice for helping your child, which I've paraphrased here from our conversations together.

1. Be empathetic. Listen deeply and walk in your child's shoes. Let your children know you understand how they feel from their perspective.

2. Keep your feelings and judgments to yourself. This is about them, *not* about you. Do not blame them. It's not their fault.

3. Refuse to bash the coach. You might feel angry about the coach's decision, but hold these feelings and talk to the coach at another time without your child present.

4. Help your child turn this experience into something positive. Point out how this situation, getting cut, does not make her or him a failure. Mention how this setback can be the foundation for future success. Relate the story of Michael Jordan to your child.

5. Encourage your child to continue to pursue other dreams, other sports, and other activities. Many individual sports, like cross country, track, tennis, and golf, rarely cut kids.

6. Disclose your own failures to your child. Personally, I like to inform my kids about my struggles, failures, setbacks, and losses and how I turned them into opportunities. Be a good role model for failure. This is modeling success.

I encourage you to hold on to this thought: there is nothing like a good failure or setback to build strong character, self-esteem, and confidence. My successes are all the results of my failures. Like Michael Jordan, I was also cut from my high school basketball team, and I believe that many of my accomplishments and much of my achievement and drive has been the result of that experience. That embarrassment propelled me to where I am today, at the top of my game.

So This Is College Recruiting?

Nothing great was ever achieved without enthusiasm.

— Ralph Waldo Emerson

Is my teenager really being recruited? How do I know? How do I do the right things and avoid silly mistakes? Being on the radar of college coaches is the dream of most high school athletes. They have worked hard and sacrificed much time just for the opportunity to receive the ultimate prize, a college scholarship. I have experienced this process from both sides: as the father of star high school athletes as well as a professional working with college coaching staffs to help them screen and select the right kids for their program.

However, let me begin by giving you a wider perspective. Whether your child is a ten-year-old prodigy you think is destined for collegiate or pro greatness or your high school senior is being actively scouted, caution is in order. The recruiting numbers are not in your favor. In no way do I want to discourage you and your kid because almost all high school athletes who work hard, perform at high levels, and have good grades certainly can be a candidate for and have a decent shot of playing in college.

That said, only about 6.7 percent of all high school athletes who go to college play at the D1, D2, D3, and NAIA levels. Only 1.7 percent of those high school athletes receive a scholarship, and that is rarely a "full ride." So as you can see, only the best of the best get the prize. Many athletes go to a university and get the chance to "walk on," having received no financial aid, but success making the team is not common.

What should you do if you think your kid is being recruited? In my experience, the process is often confusing, overwhelming, and uncertain. Kids and their parents often have a hard time figuring out how serious a college coach's interest really is. For instance, an athlete can gain the interest of a coach, but the coach may not necessarily be actively recruiting the player. Sometimes a coach will send a letter of interest to a hopeful athlete, but this is more for the coach's benefit: the coach wants to keep as many names on the recruitment list as possible, and then try to keep second-choice candidates on hold until decisions are made with others. A coach might also send a questionnaire, which is positive and shows interest, but this is also not active recruitment. Even if a college coach calls the child's high school coach, this is a good sign but not real recruiting. Don't be misled. If any of these happen, your kid has been noticed, but that's only the initial phase.

Things heat up, and get more serious, if a coach calls two or more times. Then you know he or she is really interested in recruiting the player. Some coaches will call once and that's all. If asked about their lack of interest, they will say they didn't get a good feeling about the "fit." It's all about the "fit," nothing personal. However, if a coach comes to watch the child perform, this is a sure sign of high interest. Finally, if the coach invites the child for an official visit, there's no doubt: this is a definite sign that the athlete is wanted. I experienced this entire process with one of my sons, who eventually received a scholarship offer from several colleges.

Of course, the evaluation process goes both ways. Parents and athletes need to visit schools and decide where they'd like to go, and for more than the sports programs. In addition, an entire industry has developed to help high school athletes promote themselves to college recruiters, with videos and so on. Below are several important things you should know about navigating this recruiting process as a mindful sports parent:

- First and foremost, coaches really dislike the "helicopter" mom or the "we" dad. Overzealous sports parents turn off college coaches, who see a future filled with problems. Coaches love kids who are proactive and take the initiative. That doesn't mean parents should be laissez-faire. They can help in the background, making sure their child is on track and staying organized. But let your child do the bulk of the work. Let your athlete make calls, send texts and emails, and make decisions.

- Start the process early and visit as many schools as possible, ones that are in the scope of your child's abilities. Stretch with a few and have a couple of safety-valve schools. But do begin early, perhaps in freshman or sophomore year for many sports; talk with the coach, teachers, and guidance counselors to get a sense about your child's potential.

- As early as your child's sophomore year in high school, it can be a good idea to produce a DVD of your child performing. Make a short, three-to-four-minute video of playing highlights. You could also post this on YouTube and instruct coaches how to locate it. If you are on an unofficial visit to a college, there's nothing wrong with stopping by the coach's office, introducing yourself, and leaving your video and media package. A media package includes any and all recognition of your child in sports, including newspaper stories, awards, accolades, and relevant praise about his or her abilities from those in the know. This package is like your child's sports resume.

- It is not necessary to spend a ton of money on a recruiting service. These services attempt to make the recruiting process less intimidating for parents, but they are expensive, and you can't be certain the job will get done. Your basic video and profile should suffice.

- Whatever your situation, going to college is primarily an academic decision. Be sure that the school you choose is academically viable and attractive. If you choose a school for the coach, remember that coaches sometimes leave. Choose a school your child will still love even if athletics don't work out. Ideally, the ultimate choice includes both good academics and athletic opportunities.

- High school athletes improve their chances of being recruited if they have good grades. Coaches love kids who have both high grades and lots of talent. Good grades will help to secure academic scholarship money, and this makes students more desirable to any coach. If coaches can recruit an athlete for less money, that helps their athletic budget and serves the program. Also, coaches tend to regard smart kids as less of a problem overall, on and off the field.

- In an age when so many young people feel entitled, most coaches understand the reality of families wanting to get something from the process. I know many, many head coaches in college, and every one of them, while wanting to meet your needs, is in awe of the kid who enthusiastically tells them, "I want to come here to contribute and give my all to this program." Of course, you want to get something, too, but I encourage young athletes to focus mainly on expressing to the coach their sincere desire to give to the team and the program.

- Ultimately, parents and young athletes should make the final decision together. Just because a college coach makes an offer to a student athlete doesn't mean the family will be able to afford that college. Ideally, if financial issues and other family concerns are addressed, then the ultimate decision can be made by your child.

The Sportsmanship Way

Relationships with others must not lose sight of human nature. We are more alike than different. To not grasp this we lose compassion, become moralistic, lose tolerance, become dogmatic and judgmental, and create favorites.

— Chinese wisdom

G ood sportsmanship is essential. When we don't uphold it, we lose sight of more than the game. We forget the inherent benevolence of human nature. We forget the single most basic truth for all humanity: we are more alike than different. We lose our ability to meet others heart to heart and see in everyone the same gentle, loving, kind goodness. Good sportsmanship is present when we treat everyone — athletes, coaches, officials, and yes, even parents on the opposing team — as on the same side and gathering for the same purpose, to enjoy sports. Poor sportsmanship is present when we lose compassion and tolerance and treat others as opponents and antagonists who stand in our way. When this happens, we act dogmatically and judgmentally, and we sacrifice the pure joy of the athletic experience for "winning."

What is good sportsmanship? I believe it is a spiritual concept steeped in the deep caverns of our souls. It is a heart-directed group of behaviors that include compassion, commitment, patience, respect, trust, integrity, tolerance, love, belief, caring, giving, understanding, humor, selflessness, detachment, and gratefulness...to name a few. Good sportsmanship refers to specific actions, but it is also a state of "being," in which everyone respects one another as well as respects the game. It includes the Golden Rule: treating others as you yourself would like to be treated.

Good sportsmanship means playing by the rules. No whining or drama over the outcome, and no gloating in victory. It means respecting the officials, who are doing the best they can, and accepting their judgment calls without arguing. It means watching what you say: keeping trash-talking to a minimum, if it's done at all, and avoiding emotional or profane outbursts when you are frustrated. It means cheering good plays by either team and making no excuses for bad plays or losses. It means not fighting with others and listening to and supporting the adults in charge. If there is a controversial issue, wait until later to address it with respect.

Being a good sport is not easy, but it has a positive impact on all of life for you and your child. Parents teach children proper behavior and model for kids how to act and behave. Setting the example is crucial. It means keeping one's perspective — realizing the game's larger purpose, which is to teach positive life-enhancing behavior, so that our children grow to become adults and parents who also embody good sportsmanship. According to Native American tradition, wise parents teach through being what they teach. Or as Gandhi put it: "Be the change you want to see." This higher road is the sole purpose of the game itself.

Having a calm, relaxed demeanor, being poised when others are scattered, keeping your balance with a strong sense of equanimity while all around you is a turbulent storm, this is the sportsmanship way. To manage yourself is to truly manage and mentor your children. Soft is, indeed, strong. May we all be "good sports."

My Child Is Quitting?

Quitting is not giving up, it's choosing to focus your attention on something more important....It's realizing that there are more valuable ways you can spend your time....Quitting is letting go of things (or people) that are sucking the life out of you so you can do more things that will bring you strength.

— Osayi Osar-Emokpae

One day, almost inevitably, most children will decide they want to quit a team or sport. They may have played and loved the sport for years, but now they are done. As their parent, what should you do? Do you let them quit or push them to continue?

This is perhaps the most challenging decision you and your child will confront in athletics. In fact, the reality is that most kids end their athletic careers early. One statistic is that 75 percent of the 33 million kids in sports today will drop out by the age of thirteen. By the age of eighteen, another huge number will be gone. The reasons for this are many: loss of interest, lack of enjoyment, coach and parent pressure to excel, too much time involved, lack of playing time, wanting more time to study, coaches playing favorites, burnout, and more.

For some reason, we often treat quitting a sport as a big deal, but by the age of thirteen, kids have often quit many other activities with no fanfare or issues. They just change direction and try other activities. Adults do this all the time: we change jobs, quit fitness programs, revise living arrangements, move to other locations, and change our priorities and our minds. Usually, all of this is regarded as positive. We make conscious decisions based on solid reasons. Then a child wishes to change an activity like sports, and we call it quitting, a pejorative judgment that creates stress, anxiety, and fear.

I believe it's time to embrace a more mindful approach to sports commitments. There are healthier, less-shameful ways to cope with a child who changes or ends his or her involvement in sports. We should, as the quote above states, regard quitting as a conscious choice to let go of what is no longer fun or inspiring "so you can do more things that will bring you strength."

In the big picture, what's important is supporting our children and — with patience, understanding, kindness, and encouragement — helping them find their way through such difficult choices. The key is LUV, an acroym I use to refer to listen, understand, and validate their feelings. The Chinese wisdom embodied by the Tao states that whenever we face adversity, we should pause, look, and listen to our inner voice before acting, then behave accordingly. Meanwhile, everyday parental wisdom reminds us that it is futile to try to control, push, manipulate, or force our kids to do or be what we believe is best for them. Force, as we know, creates counterforce, and kids are famous for their resistance to adult pressure.

That said, I admit that I have certainly been guilty of trying to never let my kids quit sports under any circumstance. Over the years, I have softened my approach and tried to listen first to my kid's feelings and reasons for quitting. This actually became a stronger and more effective approach. I learned to reframe quitting and treat it as an opportunity for my children to make a well-thought-out decision to walk a better path, not unlike when we quit a job we don't enjoy in favor of pursuing work we truly love. Here is an example of how I handled this situation with my son Sean when he wanted to quit basketball at the age of fifteen.

Sean is an awesome athlete, and he had been dribbling a ball from the age of three, loving every bounce. He would even take the ball to bed at night. So you can imagine how confused I was when he decided to end his romance with his first love. Thankfully, I was mindful enough to demonstrate right action, and it worked out well.

One morning, Sean came to breakfast and shocked the family with his announcement that he would no longer be playing hoops. At that time, he was his high school team's best point guard, and he was good enough to possibly play collegiately. Clearly, something serious was bothering Sean, so serious that he was ready to give up a sport I strongly believed he should stick with. But at the table, I put aside my concerns and used my LUV strategy: I listened to Sean's reasons, so I could understand his perspective, and then I validated what he felt. I asked Sean some questions about what brought this on and why he felt quitting was the best decision. Sean mentioned that he was burned out, and he was having

conflicts with several teammates. I then validated Sean's reasons
by saying, "You make solid points. I like that."

Then I asked, "Have you thought of taking a few days to mull
it over and notice how you feel next week?" Fortunately, Sean was
open to that and he agreed to wait. The following week, Sean approached me and said, "Hey Dad, I don't get out of practice till
six. Can you pick me up?" After practice, Sean told me that he'd
decided to stay on the team. That week, before making his final
decision, he had taken the time to notice the pros and cons, and
discuss them with me, to better understand his own rationale behind quitting. He looked at what he'd give up and what he'd gain,
either way. Armed with this list, the decision became clear. In the
end, my LUV strategy enabled Sean to feel accepted and respected,
and this helped him get personally clear about the right thing to
do. His choice was validated further the following year, when he
was very happy to be part of his high school team as they won
the California state championship. To this day Sean continues to
play basketball, now on a city league team, and he loves being the
head boy's basketball coach at a Colorado high school. In 2016, he
guided his team to the state championship game only to come up
short by a few points.

As a parent, I encourage you to assume that your child's decision to quit is steeped in goodness with pure intention. Their
intention is to choose something more important, a better way to
spend their time. Using LUV as a starting point, help your child
create a list of pros and cons, then you both will have a better
understanding of what is driving the desire to quit. If your child
wants to quit in midseason, I also encourage you to raise the impact that the decision will have on others. Ask your athlete: "What

effect will quitting have on your team?" And, "How do you feel about that?" Children must learn to be mindful of others and to take responsibility and be accountable for the consequences of their actions.

When handled this way, the "crisis" of quitting a sport can become an opportunity for kids to learn valuable life lessons that will benefit them for years to come. This is an awesome teaching opportunity for parents to use sport as a microcosmic classroom for life.

Confucius says, "The great leader guides others and does not pull them along; urges them to go forward by opening the way, yet refuses to take them to the place." Quitting a sport is not an end. It is a beginning based on a good decision that opens new directions to go forward. So help guide, nudge, and support your little stars to move forward with another sport or fun activity if what they are doing now no longer brings them joy.

Approaching the Coach

I speak to everyone in the same way, whether he is the garbage man or the president of the university.

— Albert Einstein

Your son is not being played for reasons you do not know. Your daughter is taken out of a game without explanation. Your son is playing a position on the court that doesn't match his abilities. Your daughter is "called out" for making one mistake. You want to talk with the coach to understand why, but should you? There are many valid reasons for a parent to approach a coach, but if this conversation isn't handled mindfully, it has the potential for creating an even worse situation.

The parent-coach relationship is delicate. It takes skill to approach a coach and maximize the chances for positive results. Typically, a parent wants the coach to make a change or act differently. However, coaches usually have reasons for the way things are. For the parent, the best approach is to propose or create a

win-win scenario, where you work with the coach to find a mutually satisfying, respectful solution to the problem. The following
are a few assertive, mindful ways to accomplish this goal.

1. If at all possible, have your child approach the coach.
   You want your child to get the message that he or she can
   take care of him- or herself, even in situations involving a
   coach. You might want to ask your child what he or she is
   feeling about the issues at hand. It may be different than
   how you feel, and if so, respect those feelings, even if it
   means leaving the situation alone. Also, if it's a onetime
   issue, let it go.

2. Avoid emails, phone calls, and, of course, texting. When
   you talk, choose a place that is neutral, quiet, and free
   of distraction. Be sure to make good eye contact and be
   aware of maintaining positive body language and other
   nonverbal cues. Be mindful to keep a respectful tone in
   your voice.

3. Once you have spoken and described your issue, listen
   and ask nonthreatening questions to better understand
   the coach's perspective. Reflect back to the coach what he
   or she is saying to show that you understand the explanation. If you remain unclear, ask the coach to clarify. Making the effort to understand the coach's perspective sets
   the stage for furthering your cause and achieving your
   goal.

4. Avoid harsh criticism, personal attacks, or blame. This
   will cause the coach to get defensive and possibly aggressive. Focus on the issue or your child, not the coach. It is
   best to state how you feel and why. For example: "I feel

upset when my son is told he'll get more playing time and then he doesn't. He's becoming frustrated and losing interest in playing." Or, "I was confused when I got an unexpected bill in the mail for new fees, since I thought we agreed that the trip was going to be free of cost." Describe the problem and keep your emotions separate from the issue at hand. Blame, accusations, and attacks will not further your chances of favorable outcomes.

5. In addition to raising a problem, provide positive comments as well. This is a good way to begin a conversation. For example: "Hey, Mark, I love the way you create a positive, caring environment for the kids. They seem to really thrive with that. However, my son, Jason, is becoming confused over his playing time. You've told him he'll play more, but it hasn't happened yet. Can you explain how you're handling this, so I can help Jason understand and avoid getting frustrated?" You may want to end with another positive statement like: "Otherwise, Jason loves being on the team, especially your sense of humor. Thanks."

These strategies will help your chances of having a respectful, positive, fruitful interaction with the coach. It takes practice but it's worth it. Being mindful of how to communicate positions you and your child for potential success.

Specialization
or Diversification?

All the good hockey players seemed to play lacrosse in those days and every one of them learned something from the game to carry over to the other — things athletes can only learn by mixing up the games they play when they are young.

— Wayne Gretzky

The pressure to have your child choose a single sport and play it all year has never been stronger. Specialization in youth sport circles is a very hot and contested issue. Parents fear that their child will fall behind the other kids, not make the travel team, and lose out on scholarships if he or she is not in a highly structured, competitive environment all year, around the clock. While a few highly motivated children might benefit from specialization, I feel very strongly that a healthier, happier approach for the vast majority of kids is to diversify a child's sports experience, as Wayne Gretzky suggests.

In the introduction, I recount my early experiences with youth sports. It was so different back in those days. We'd play summer sports in winter, and spring sports in the fall, and all of them in one long day during summer. There was basketball in the morning followed by baseball, football, boxball, and before night set in, a wild, highly competitive game of "hide and seek." In high school I played three sports. Everyone was capable of and had the opportunity to play collegiately. Some chose to play at that level, others did not. Five kids from my neighborhood went on to play professional sports, including Sandy Koufax of the Dodgers. This happened without specialization. We were athletes who diversified, and when we were ready, we chose the sport that we most loved from a wide sample of activities. To this day, I hike, bike, run, and do it all with my kids.

Today, youth sports organizations have become big business, and the urge to specialize is largely driven by money, status, and greed. Scholarships dangle like carrots and obscure the value of multisport participation. Specialization, playing a single sport, has its own physical, emotional, social, and spiritual costs that are hidden by the frenzy to be the best. Specialization is a path that I believe is not in the best interests of most young athletes. Many of my professional athlete clients have told me about the importance of keeping kids well-diversified in sports. Most of them were multisport athletes, choosing to specialize around the age of sixteen. In a recent article, Urban Meyer, the head coach of the Ohio State University football team, said that he prefers to recruit athletes who played multiple sports in high school. The article mentioned that out of forty-seven athletes recruited by Meyer at OSU over a particular period of time, forty-two were multisport kids and only five specialized in football. Most of the college coaches that I have worked with over the years have been the same; they prefer athletes who diversify their sports experiences.

I would like to propose a new path for our young athletes. Listen to your inner voice. What do you, as a parent, intuitively feel is the right thing to do? What do you believe is the right path for the full emotional, mental, physical, and spiritual development of your child? What path leads to more fun and enjoyment and to less anxiety, burnout, and injury? If you can silence the frantic, fanatic voices of youth organizations, coaches, and other anxious parents, I believe you will agree that the right path is diversification, a multisport approach with less structure and stress.

Of course, not everyone agrees, and you may feel that there are compelling reasons for your child to specialize in one sport. If so, here are some further things to consider if you are experiencing self-doubt or as you weigh options with your child about this important issue. My experience tells me that the dangers of specialization far outweigh the advantages:

Psychologically, children who specialize often experience burnout by the age of thirteen or fourteen, which can result in quitting sports entirely. Increased pressure and anxiety over outcomes, results, and statistics can wear out kids mentally and even spiritually. Without the fun, they are done. Then there is the risk of kids becoming disillusioned if, after putting in all those years of hard work, they don't get the big payoff, a college scholarship. This experience impacts their self-esteem and identity, and it could result in a generalized feeling of worthlessness or depression.

Physically, overuse injuries have become quite common. Specialization leaves no time for the body to recover and rest. Most medical and chiropractic physicians recommend that kids avoid specialization, which places excessive wear and tear on these young developing bodies. One study found that, among kids who specialized, over 80 percent were more likely to be injured than kids who diversified. When overuse injuries occur, there is the potential for chronic, lifelong injuries, which can result in kids completely walking away from all physical activity.

Meanwhile, the advantages of diversification are plenty. Playing multiple sports leads to better overall physical athletic development, as well as stronger balance, more speed, and better coordination because children employ a wider range of motion and muscle use. This wide variety of athletic skill development can easily transfer to their eventual sport of choice, and as a result, this makes them better all-around athletes. All of my kids played multiple sports and excelled, and by the age of sixteen, they narrowed to one sport, their favorite.

In addition, playing multiple sports reduces the risk of injury and burnout, increases self-esteem as well as confidence, and improves the chances for long-term athletic participation well into adulthood.

However, if your child is mainly interested in only one sport, I suggest that you make sure your child still has an off-season. This will help to avoid burnout, and it enables your kid to have a fresh start when his or her sport rolls around again. During this off-season, encourage other sports or activities to ensure the development of your child's full human capacities — mentally, physically, emotionally, and spiritually.

When parents say no to early specialization, they say yes to a more-balanced, fun, fully functional sports life, one that is physically and psychologically more sound. Consider not having your child specialize until ninth grade at the earliest. Tenth grade, even better.

As a sports professional and dad, I support this. The cutting-edge research in sports science on this issue backs me up, and it feels intuitively like the right thing. Just say no!

The Sophistication of Simplicity

I do not think that any civilization can be called complete until
it has...made a conscious return to simplicity of thinking and
living.

— Lin Yutang, *The Importance of Living*

To add to this Chinese scholar's observation, the brilliant
artist Leonardo da Vinci proclaimed, "Simplicity is the
ultimate sophistication." American philosopher Ralph Waldo
Emerson said that "to be simple is to be great." In an era where
the internet has us drowning in a sea of information, these are
gentle reminders about the beauty and essentialness of simplicity.

This has never been truer for sports parenting. Kids need
simple. Parents need simple. Sport is simple, or it should be.
Don't become overwhelmed with all the concepts and advice in
this book, and don't overwhelm your children, either. Kids have
way too much coming at them as it is. Take only a couple of ideas
at a time and work with your child on them. When those are

incorporated, move on to more. The Tao says that the journey of a thousand miles begins with a single step. No need to complicate things.

The Chinese word *pu* (pronounced "poo") is translated as "the uncarved block." It is a state of simplicity and pure potential much like our children. It is a plain block, free of interference or contamination. See your child as the uncarved block, uncluttered. As athletes, they don't need to know every technique and strategy. They need to just be, to just play.

The reason I love the sport of running is its basic simplicity. You can run anytime, anywhere, with only a pair of running shoes and nothing else. In rain, shine, sleet, or snow, I can be "on the go." Yet, as simple as it is, it's also become big business with fancy watches, specialized shoes and clothes, heart monitors, hydration systems, computer chips, and more. Today, I simply run and pay no attention to this complexity. I prefer to listen to my body.

As a sports parent, look for ways to free yourself and your child from all the irrelevant and extraneous clutter of life, of what sports parenting can bring to the table. Look but don't eat. There may be several simultaneous activities available to your child. Avoid getting involved with every possibility. One sport at a time is enough. Adding more, along with other activities, will only complicate your child's life, to say nothing about your own. Simplify things by learning to say no. Saying no to one thing says yes to another . . . including to your and your child's sanity.

The journey of sport for youngsters is so simple: play, have fun, laugh, and feel the joy of being alive. The journey of a sports parent can be so simple: let them play, give the game back to them, and tell them how much you love watching them being happy.

That's all. As the *Tao Te Ching* tells us, "Know what is enough; return to simplicity."

Gratefulness as a Practice

The root of joy is gratefulness.... It is not joy that makes us grateful; it is gratitude that makes us joyful.

— Brother David Steindl-Rast

I am honored and blessed to have had several personal meetings with Brother David Steindl-Rast, a very special, wise, engaging, and humble man. On our last visit together at the Esalen Institute in Big Sur on the California coast, we talked about gratefulness and how to practice it in our daily lives. The conversation helped me to focus on my family as a huge gift rather than thinking about what was lacking and all the difficult, challenging aspects of parenting.

I sometimes feel that in the world of sports, parents fall into the trap of thinking about what's missing with their kids — they're not fast enough, big enough, strong enough, talented enough, good enough, focused enough, playing enough, recognized enough, liked enough, given enough. Enough already! It's easy to think about scarcity rather than abundance, to forget to be grateful for what we and our children have. There's so much love in our lives when we are surrounded by these little critters.

Here's a recommendation. Whenever we get caught up being sports parents, imagine being sports grandparents. See your kids as if they were your grandkids. See them through pure hearts of love, with no agendas, with nothing missing, with the only goal to watch them having fun and to participate in their youth. It's so simple but not easy.

I also recommend expressing gratefulness as a daily practice. For five minutes each day, focus on your gratitude for what you have been given, all of your blessings. Then go about the rest of your day making everything you do and how you're being a mere reflection of these gifts.

Gratefulness is the process of becoming mindful of what is genuinely important and holding that feeling in your heart. What's important to you, what you're grateful for, can change each day depending upon what comes your way. For me, certain items are more constant, as in, "I am grateful for my family, my life partner, my ability to make a difference in the lives of others through my writing and work, my healthy body, my comfortable home, my mental clarity, my sense of humor," and so on. Each day new items get added to the list.

Here's an exercise that my wife, Jan, and I practice regularly. We do this before getting out of bed, and it has the power to transform our days and impact everything we are doing and how we are being. Give this a shot and be sure to include everything that's good and special about your kids in sport.

1. Make a list of five or more items that make you feel grateful.

2. Go over the list and get connected to how these make you feel: calm, peaceful, loving, fortunate, blessed...all feelings of gratefulness.

3. Take in one deep, slow breath through your nose, and as you do, take in this feeling of gratefulness. Have the feeling surround your heart, hold your breath for four seconds, and then slowly release it.

4. Repeat this deep breathing three times.

5. Notice how relaxed and peaceful you feel. Now — go about the rest of the day and make everything a reflection of what you've been given. In other words, give back.

You will notice the difference in how you perform. The ordinary will become extraordinary. This alignment with your heart will give you a broader, richer, more meaningful perspective on all the mundane realities of your sports parenting as well as on your little stars.

Let me end with these words of wisdom from Brother David:

Look closely and you will find that people are happy because they are grateful...Everything is a gift. The degree to which we are awake to this truth is a measure of our gratefulness, and gratefulness is a measure of our aliveness...We are never more than one grateful thought away from peace of heart.

Cycles of Change

The only way to make sense out of change is to plunge into it, move with it, and join the dance.

— Alan Watts

There is only one constant in life and that is change. Things, people, and places shift and change. It's inevitable, much to my chagrin. I struggle with change until I remember how we are given what we need in order to grow, expand, and experience the fullness of life. One day you are up, winning at everything, and in the flow. The next day brings chaos and crisis, and you are down, struggling every minute that you're awake. Sometimes those tough days are essential because all things and circumstances in life are interconnected and interdependent.

Fighting these cycles is futile, and it is unhealthy. Moods shift and weather changes, as do the seasons; the moon rises and the sun sets. Change is nature, nature is change, and that fact can't be changed, regardless of how you feel about it.

As your kids play sports, so much change will happen over time. There is no straight and narrow path. Whenever I thought one of my kids had settled into an athletic endeavor, change happened: with them, with their teams, with their opportunities. Our family's sports life has always been challenging, and we've had a difficult time with all the change.

The change that you and your child experience on this journey will be mostly inner shifts, and they will ripple outward to all aspects of your life. I cannot suggest what to do with all this change, other than to expect it and act accordingly, using all the available data to choose wisely. However, to see the big picture, anticipate, and be flexible, we must stay *mindful* — when change happens, stop, observe, and listen to your inner voice. I hope that this book helps you to learn these skills and provides a comfortable place to lean on during times of change.

In Chinese, *I Pien* suggests that you stay awake to the universal rhythm of nature that renews itself in cyclical fashion. Notice the shifts in life and act in harmony with them, refusing to force a square peg into a round hole.

Sports kids, who are totally into athletics as a lifestyle, can wake up one morning and decide they are ready to drop out. This happened to my son Sean, and yet he changed his mind and stuck with basketball. This also happened with my son Brennan when he was a scholarship runner at the University of Colorado. One day, he decided he no longer wanted to run collegiately, and he left the team. Competitive running was no longer a good fit for him. Each made the right choice.

One thing is certain: children's bodies will change drastically, and this impacts their success and the sports they play. But also, their circle of friends will change, as will their interests outside of school, especially in the social scene. Their relationship with you will change as they experience the natural process of individuation. A time will come when they will want to put distance between you to get a better sense of independence. For years, my son Sean wouldn't leave my side, then in tenth grade, he didn't have the time of day for me. Then at the age of twenty-two, he came back to me, and at the age of twenty-seven, he and I have become good friends enjoying each other's company. All of my kids have gone through these stages of vast change, of connection and separation. I haven't liked it one bit. But in time, all our relationships became wonderful again.

I always tell the story to my clients and audiences about the mythological phoenix, which consumes itself by fire, burning up, and yet a new young bird springs from its ashes, quickly rising up, expressing exuberance for a new, changed life.

This is the difficult truth for you as a sports parent of an athletic child. Whether you do or don't like the way things are right now, know that they will change, and then they will change again.

PART FOUR

Code of Conduct

Giving the Game Back to Them

Be the Wise Grandparent

I have learned that kids need distance once the game or match ends. On the ride home, children prefer to let the game stay at the ballpark and to be in the moment. Be like a wise sage or grandparent and just tell them how you love watching them play. Let your child initiate a sports discussion. Athletics are their thing, not yours. Let them determine where the conversation goes. This way you demonstrate trust, respect, and positive regard for your child. You might want to simply ask — now that the game is over, is there anything about it that you'd like to discuss? Your kids will appreciate that they are in the "driver's seat" even if they're sitting in the back of the car.

Know Your Role

Know your role. Every code-of-conduct item in part 4 is meant to help you understand your primary role. You are a sports parent. And yet each sport has only four kinds of participants: coaches, athletes, officials, and spectators. Which are you? That's right, a sports-parent spectator. During games and practices, if you do more than watch, or you spectate in a way that embarrasses your child, it is you who must change your approach. When you change the way you look at things, the things you look at change. It took me a little while and much prompting from my kids to realize that I am not the coach or the official. My role is to be the best sports parent I can be and simply love watching them play.

Use *You*, Not *We*

D rop the word *we* when referring to your child's sports journey. For example, don't say, "We practiced that for weeks," or "We have a game tomorrow." Watch out for statements that attempt to share credit for a victory: "You played just like I showed you," and "We beat them convincingly." Pay attention to your pronouns, and strike out *we*. It's their game, so give it back to them.

Detach from Outcome

Teach children the ancient Buddhist principle of "letting go," which will be valuable to them in all aspects of life for as long as they live. Detachment from outcomes and results is the true path of ultimate happiness. Paradoxically, when you let go of an attachment to winning, you experience achievement. When children focus on simply competing (or the process), they experience less anxiety and play better. This results in what I call the inner invisible victory. When children set and meet personal standards or goals, they feel satisfaction and pride no matter the game outcome. Point out this concept anytime a child says he or she enjoyed playing, even in defeat.

Another approach is to talk about the concept of pride. I often reminded my kids when they were young to play in a way that enabled them to feel proud. Prior to a performance, I encouraged them to ask themselves the question, "What can I do that will enable me to feel good about myself and give me a strong sense of pride?" Children can answer aloud or to themselves, but their response will direct their behavior during the event. This is a valuable focusing technique to help children "park" their attention on the process and experience this invisible victory within.

Ask about Feelings, Not Performance

I always try to remember that we are human beings, not "human doings." Most of the world of sports is intent upon doing, expecting others to do rather than be. Therefore, at the conclusion of each game or practice, I tried to ask my kids, "How did you feel?" rather than "How did you do?" The first is a process-oriented question, and the second focuses on outcome, production, and results. By asking about feelings, my goal is always to create a safe environment for a deeper conversation in which a child can evaluate the game, their play, and how they performed, rather than focusing on a win or loss. To me, these lessons are the true purpose of the event, and this conversation is where those truths and wisdom can be discovered and expressed. In this giving, fluid, soulful talk, parents listen first and learn what they need to know to help their child learn from the experience. Most of us assume we know, when, indeed, it is the child who knows. This is what it means to adopt a Zen "beginner's mind."

Teach Excellence, Not Winning

Teach children a different concept of winning. Encourage them to see each competitive event as an opportunity to display their skills against other well-prepared athletes. Winning in this sense is about executing the process beautifully and brilliantly. When we focus first on achieving excellence, we force ourselves to dig down deep inside to discover what we are made of. This effort is itself a skill that we can later call upon in times of need. When children have outstanding performances, but they or their team loses, remind them to take pride in their own performance and in their effort to achieve excellence. After all, prizes, medals, wins, and other external rewards are transitory. Excellence lasts a lifetime; it's forever. When athletes compete and focus on doing well with what they can control — defensive play, their work ethic, their attitude, their preparation — they achieve what I call true winning.

Honor the Game

Honor the game for what it is: a positive culture that contributes fun to our children's lives, where they can learn positive character traits that will pay dividends twenty or thirty years down the road as they become well-adjusted citizens because of this amazing experience with athletics. Be grateful for what sports have to offer each day — the games our kids play in sports.

Go with the Flow

D o not force your child to participate in athletics. Give your
kids the choice to play or not to play. If a child is involved
with an activity that he or she would rather not do, the outcome
can become a disaster, not just for the child but for the team, the
coach, and you as well. Remember the Chinese principle of *wu
wei*: seek the effortless effort of nonforce. Going with the flow is
essential for your happiness and that of your child. When your
child wants to end a sport, treat him or her with LUV: listen, understand by asking questions, and validate his or her feelings.

Avoid Game Debriefings

After a game, do not feel compelled to always discuss what happened. Kids care about playing games, but they want to talk about other important things in their lives, too. They don't like "game debriefings." Kids want relief from sports talk after a game, not an interview.

However, if you do discuss sports, ask your kids process-oriented questions that focus on their athletic experience. For example: What was the best part of today's game? What did you learn from playing today? What did the coach talk about after the game? What went well for you? What is it about the game today that you wish you could change? Notice how all these questions require something more than a yes or no response. In this way, you encourage your child to be more engaged. However, if your child doesn't want to talk about the game, be respectful of his or her feelings. Simply say, "I really enjoyed watching you play," and change the topic.

Love Them Regardless
of How They Play

Don't treat your child one way after a loss and another way following a win. Kids are very sensitive to this, as you, I, and anyone would be. Children will begin to think that parental love is conditional, that it is tied to the outcome of games or their performance. When my kids were young, I often reassured them that I loved them regardless of how they played.

Win or lose, be consistent. If you have trouble with this, it may be because you are taking your children's successes and failures personally. Recall the story I told earlier about the female athlete whose father stopped coming to her games because she wasn't playing well. His self-worth had become connected to her performance, and this eventually destroyed his relationship with his daughter. To this day, she avoids being in his company...and he wonders why.

Lighten Up

Believe it or not, the most important aspect of sports for kids is to have fun; winning is secondary, especially for very young children. Taoist scholar Alan Watts once said that "man suffers only because he takes seriously what the gods made for fun." Parents lose sight of this and superimpose their own need to win over their children's need to have fun. Parents who become overly enthusiastic about the outcome of games pass this frenetic attitude directly on to their kids. We lose sight of the fun factor and take our children and sports too seriously. I believe, if we were to ask them, our children would tell us to "lighten up." To test this notion, ask your child, "When you play a game, would you rather have fun and lose or not have fun and win?" Listen closely to the answer and go with their flow, and if necessary, find ways to modulate your zealous enthusiasm for your child's athletic experiences. Being listened to is very much the same as being loved. And this is what kids crave.

Listen, Don't Fix

Parents often feel they need to protect children from setbacks, errors, or failure in sports. When a child experiences such outcomes, it is best to simply be present and actively listen to his or her feelings. Ask questions and provide words of comfort that help children get in touch with what's going on, such as saying, "You seem disappointed," or "How are you feeling?" or "It's no fun to lose." Statements like these demonstrate to children that you care, understand, and want to know how they feel. Avoid trying to "fix it" by saying things like, "You'll get them next time," or "It's not important; it doesn't matter." Any attempts to avoid or cover up true feelings only serve to remind children of the loss even more deeply. By asking about and listening to their feelings, you allow children to express themselves, and this helps them naturally recover and get on with the business of having fun. Children learn from their losses and eventually forge ahead. Praise effort. You can offer praise for playing fairly and giving their all. Indeed, for me, when children do their best to be their best, that is winning.

Be Totally Present

In my experience, kids enjoy having parents attend their sporting events. I still remember the disappointed look on the face of my son when I once told him I'd be away for one of his games. In fact, I decided right then and there that, from then on, all of my professional travel would take place between Sunday and Friday, leaving Saturday open during soccer and basketball seasons. What my children didn't appreciate was me showing up and, instead of watching the game, socializing with the other parents or talking on a cell phone. My children always wanted my full attention on their passionate efforts on the field or court; they wanted me to watch as they performed like champions. In essence, my children were encouraging me to be mindful, to find joy in the present moment, to feel alive and be with life as it was happening. So, practice mindfulness at your child's games: Observe your surroundings, the activity going on, the atmosphere, and most of all the happiness of your child. Be totally present. This is how you truly live mindfully. Children may say it's fine when a parent misses a game, and they may be sincere, but that doesn't change what their heart really wants. Trust me! Listen to your child's heart, and watch them play.

Be a Parent, Not a Coach

Most kids do not want to hear advice from a parent, particularly just prior to, during, or just after a game. This can be true even if the parent is also the coach. In some situations, a parent has the expertise and has acted as a "mentor-coach" from the time his or her child began to play sports. If this describes your relationship, you may find your child receptive to your coaching advice, but this is not a common situation. Most children would prefer that parents not offer advice, however accurate or well-intentioned.

If you'd like to offer playing advice, let your child be the one to initiate this. Say, "If you want my help, let me know. I'm here for you." Then wait and listen for their request. Demonstrate patience, and resist the urge to give the advice anyway. Your child will make it clear what is needed and when. Following this advice has not been easy for me, but I have tried to practice it often. Instead of giving advice, encourage your young athlete to approach the coach with important questions about how to play. Typically, advice that might be vehemently resisted coming from you as the parent might be embraced coming from the coach. Coaches look upon this favorably; this is in the best interest of the child. Your job as a sports parent is to simplify, not complicate what already is. Advice isn't helpful if it isn't accepted. Avoid offering answers and opinions and stick to listening.

Be Seated, Please

D o not pace back and forth on the sidelines. Your child will sense that you are anxious, and that will cause him or her to feel nervous and get distracted. Remain seated in the stands, without your smartphone or tablet, and enjoy the event and what it teaches your child. Pay attention to what you intuitively know is right. Be sensitive and aware of the context. Actually, the game itself is not what's important. What matters is the game within the game. Focus on how the game of sport creates an opportunity for the game within, for the joy, excitement, and fun that sports provide for these youngsters.

Respect the Coaches
and Officials

In every interaction with coaches, officials, and referees, express gratitude for their involvement and praise for their work. Emphasize truthful positive statements even if you disagree with some things they may have done. Oftentimes, the adults who run youth sports just hear from parents when they have complaints and negative statements, when they are venting frustration and disappointment. Let coaches and officials run the event without interference, and let them know what they've done well. After all, their rewards are certainly not financial, as few youth coaches or officials get paid much, if anything.

At the beginning of a season, make it a point to meet the coach and offer assistance if needed. Establish a positive relationship with the other adults who are running the team, which will help to shape a positive experience for your child, and for the other athletes as well. Then, if conflict arises later, you have laid a foundation of respect and trust. As a parent, focus on giving and serving. Give the gift of kindness, of assistance, of connection, and of your time. Remember to never undermine the coach or others, which causes havoc for everyone.

Let the Coach Run the Team

In accordance with doing the right thing, avoid all talk with a coach about your child's playing time or playing position, overall team strategy, or other players on the team. Coaches have told me that they are often approached by parents with these issues. Let your coach run the team, and help your athlete to focus on what is within his or her control. For example, your child can work hard, help clean up after practice, and set performance goals with the help of the coach. The latter will help them increase the chances of more playing time or a clearer role on the team. If you are concerned with your child's behavior, certainly discuss that with the coach — for instance, if your child is expressing frustration or is becoming discouraged. If a coach asks you for your input, don't hesitate to give it. Otherwise, it would be best to let the coach do the coaching and remember that you are simply a spectator.

Avoid Freaking Out over Injuries

There are two kinds of athletes: those who get injured and those who will get injured. That said, youngsters rarely get seriously injured, even in sports like gymnastics and football, where growing incidents of concussions are a genuine concern. Sports injuries have increased overall, and one major reason is specialization.

When the moment arrives that you see your kid go down, temper the panic that inevitably arises. Breathe and wait on the sidelines until the coach checks out your child. If it's serious, the coach will call you over. Otherwise, unless your child starts screaming for you, don't go out on the field or the floor. Kids can easily become embarrassed by parents freaking out when something happens to them. If you race to your child's side, and it turns out to be nothing, your child may become angry and scared. Be confident and optimistic, and listen carefully, both in the moment and afterward.

Ground All Helicopters

Don't hang around the playing field, practice arena, or close to the bench so that you can give your kid some tips to improve his or her performance. This is embarrassing for your child. Plus, it distracts from the coach's instructions, and your child might get confused if what you say differs from the coach. I remember when one of my athletic sons asked me to not show up at practices anymore, and I was a bit put off by that request. However, I listened and obliged, and my son became happier, more relaxed, and played at higher levels according to his coach. Remember this: When you are in tune with the way things work, then they work the way they need to, no matter what you think or do at the time. The urge to "helicopter" can be well-intentioned; we are trying to help our kids from making a mistake. Then again, this may prevent our child from learning vital lessons that, once learned, could help him or her perform best of all. Sports create opportunities for kids to grow, mature, and develop as fine human beings. This happens without our involvement, contrary to what many of us believe. If you start to hover, ground that helicopter. There is one caveat, however, and that is if the coach asks parents to help, feel free to volunteer and help in that way. But even then, let your kid play without any "helpful" suggestions.

Don't Yell at the Ref

I once overheard a twelve-year-old soccer player tell her dad, "You're always telling me to behave, yet you yell at the ref. That's embarrassing to me. I don't like it." Dad took a deep breath and said, "You're right; I'm sorry." To his credit, the man apologized to the ref after the game as his daughter stood by his side. By listening to her message and respecting the referee, he saved the day and looked good in the eyes of everyone. In the process, he strengthened within his daughter the importance of good behavior by modeling what he expected from her as a player. Soccer gave this dad the opportunity to learn a lesson for life, much like the game does for these young athletes.

Cheer Properly

Surprisingly, most kids do not want their parents cheering just for them. They want encouragement and support for themselves and their team. Cheering properly is a delicate balance. Yelling can embarrass children, while applause at the appropriate moment or timely, gentle comments like "nice play" or "good shot" are what kids say feel good. If you're unsure what your own child prefers, ask. Don't let cheering interfere with your child's concentration; let things evolve naturally. Listen to what kids want and don't want.

Display Affection Appropriately

Outward displays of affection on the field in front of others are usually not appreciated by young athletes. As with anything in nature, kids need and want affection, but save outward expressions of parental love for when the game or event is completed. If your child approaches you affectionately, follow his or her lead. Otherwise, be aware that this is an issue and use your intuitive best judgment about how to display affection appropriately. As with all things, look for the flow in all of life, and when you notice it, act accordingly.

Be the Change You Want to See

Be a model of good behavior for your children. For example, while at the game, demonstrate the poise, calm, control, confidence, respect, trust, and integrity you expect of them. As Gandhi once said: "Be the change you want to see." Encourage your child to do as you do. For example, if you would like your child to experience what it's like to meditate, practice meditation on a consistent basis yourself. If you hope that your child can embrace failure as a teacher, demonstrate the ways that you learn from your own setbacks and loss. Sport is a microcosmic classroom for learning lessons for life. If we want to teach our children to do what is right, we must be what we wish to teach. In sports and in all of life, if we model natural human goodness, we help create a balanced, harmonious daily life.

Epilogue:
Way of the Expansive Spirit

A new philosophy, a new way of life, is not given for nothing. It is acquired with much patience and great effort.

— Fyodor Dostoyevsky

I love how Eastern thought and Native American tradition emphasize the essential goodness in all children. The Tao calls this essential goodness the *way of the expansive spirit*. The purpose of this book is to help us align with this concept, to help us protect, guard, and maintain this spirit, the goodness in these young athletes, not just in sport but for all of life. Our work is to guide our kids to discover this goodness within themselves and to help them to become more mindful and to awaken to who they are and ultimately what they can be. When given this powerful opportunity, they will perform well in all arenas of life. Oftentimes we make the mistake of forcing or coercing our children into a direction that they resent, and as a result they offer counterforce. Preserving the inner goodness in our kids is a delicate process.

Such a process of nurturing the expansive spirit in your children can be accomplished by supporting your kids' dreams, helping them to "think big" when it's realistically possible. Timely, valuable feedback can help them to gain proper perspective. Truth and honesty must be strictly adhered to. Be sure to communicate often your belief in your kids and watch their confidence rise. With an open mind and heart to the passions, wishes, and desires of your children, you can help guide them softly in their chosen directions. In this process, each child discovers greatness within, holds on to his or her expansive spirit, and believes, indeed, that "I did it myself."

When you engage in the process described throughout this book, you and your child can grow and expand to feel free, alive, positive, energetic, and strong. It is a way of true liberation — physically, mentally, emotionally, and spiritually. In such a dynamic, spiritual relationship, you and your child never stop growing and expanding as you are both gently "pushed" safely into waters you once feared.

This is not unlike when a young child first learns to swim. A parent, standing in shallow water at the edge of the pool, implores his or her three-year-old son to jump. The boy may say, "No, I'm scared." The parent again encourages the boy, who inches up to the edge but doesn't go in. Again, the parent gently asks the child to jump, saying, "I will protect you. It's fun." Then the boy jumps and screams with incredible joy.

This book, *Let Them Play*, presents numerous specific behaviors, qualities, characteristics, and attributes that contribute to a healthy choreographed dance between sports parent and athletic child while preserving the child's expansive spirit. This relationship is open, compassionate, and caring, and it exudes passion and inspiration for personal growth. A wise parent supports the dreams and goals of the child while being aware of the problematic tendency for parents to live vicariously through their children. Mindful parents provide much validation and affirmation of the child, which promotes self-reliance, confidence, and self-actualization in the young athlete. Your faith in your child helps to reduce fear and anxiety in times of chaos and crisis. In a loving, compassionate, safe environment, your child can step away and risk failure, knowing that setbacks are simply lessons that help guide the way. While it may be unreasonable to expect any of us to function at this level all of the time, our heightened awareness of this approach will certainly raise the percentage of time that we function, teach, and guide from this sacred perspective. However, with courage, compassion, and respect, adults can make these changes for our children and learn to simply *let them play*.

The Courage to Change

It takes courage to take the risk to make the changes suggested in this book. It is the same courage that you ask from your kids as they embark on their journey of playing sports. Know that this change is a challenge yet is refreshingly rewarding. You follow this vision by following your heart, believing that such a shift is what your child wants, needs, and craves. This is a very special and exciting time to be a sports parent. We are truly blessed with a vital calling to create safe environments where our children feel free to open their hearts; only then can we step inside and help them to believe they can be something other than ordinary.

When sports parenting is aligned with the principles of the Tao, the more natural way, we become more humble, kind, nonjudgmental, intuitive, and selfless. We encourage positive focus and direction by modeling a more effective, enlightened style of parenting — one where cooperation and partnership are honored for the purposes of human dignity; one where you belong to the youth sports culture rather than own it; one where you and your child can blossom to your full human potential in an environment of unconditional positive regard. The wisdom and lessons in this book aim to guide and lead you to fulfilling such a vision for your athletic child.

This courage is truly selfless. To paraphrase the *Tao Te Ching*:

> With good sports parents
> When their work is done
> Their task fulfilled
> The children will all feel that
> They have done it themselves.

Taking the First Step

The journey to parent more mindfully is just beginning, and it holds the key to much joy, success, and fulfillment. But as Dostoyevsky reminds us, this path requires much patience and great effort. It takes work, and work takes time. Start gradually with small increments at first. Earlier I used the example that "the journey of a thousand miles begins with a single step." Focus on each step, until the steps add up to a daily practice, and soon enough you will experience the rewards of progress.

Unlike most sojourns, which start and end at a predetermined destination, the beauty of this journey is that it is never ending. We will continually experience new and exciting sacred beginnings and positive change over the course of our entire life. When we shift our attitudes and beliefs about what is possible in our parenting, we redefine our potential, which is unlimited. We discover, as I mentioned earlier, that there is no path to mastery; mastery is the path. It's a day-to-day proposition where we continually self-improve and blossom as parents, as people, and become strong in all phases of our life. As the *Tao Te Ching* says, "Those who master themselves have strength."

Sports parenting is an art — the art of selflessly serving and guiding softly while extending trust and respect to our children. Firmness through gently worded directives and commands will give our kids a sense of self-worth and belonging. They will tend to be more productive and play more optimally when we guide rather than rule them. This selfless, serving approach is a way to gain their trust and respect. To quote the *I Ching*:

> Kindness and service toward others will create a spirit of unparalleled loyalty. They will take upon themselves... hardship and sacrifice toward the attainment of goals. It is necessary that you have firmness, selflessness, and correctness within, and an encouraging attitude toward those you guide.

In this book, I have attempted to create a mindful guide for sports parenting. I hope you find this book a reliable and faithful companion as you travel and enjoy this never-ending journey. Indeed, as you make your way along this path of wisdom, I encourage you to go beyond what I offer and create your own strategies.

I mean this book as a guide, not a doctrine. Its purpose is to point your feet in a positive direction and to present a broader perspective on the delicate art of parenting athletic kids. This path offers many lessons in spiritual growth, and it can become a way of bringing families closer together. As I always tell young athletes, focus on the process, not the results, and the results will come. Or as Cervantes once said, "The journey is better than the inn." Your kids are only young for a short time; they grow up so fast. Make the most of it.

Remember, finally, to see the humor in all of this sacred work. Maybe the biggest parenting mistake you can make is to treat inner growth and change as serious business. Spirituality and laughter are not mutually exclusive. It is said that the Buddha awakens each day with laughter and dance, and Chinese author Lin Yutang, in his classic book *The Importance of Living*, reminds us that it is the wise soul who becomes a "laughing philosopher." Yutang notes how we take ourselves far too seriously, and he emphasizes the importance of humor in creating a happy, peaceful life. Laughter restores our perspective and keeps the heart open for doing this important, mindful, and sacred work with our youngsters. We should aim to cultivate joyful, merry laughter in all that we do.

The path that we walk when parenting athletic children is like a dancing river, moving slowly at times when faced with obstacles and blockages, only to speed up again as the terrain steepens. At times, we feel as though we are not making any progress, like the river is reversing on itself, turning in different directions, as if it has lost its compass. Yet like the river, we steadily carve out our course, creating channels that, over time, enable us to fluidly flow in the desired direction. Your path, like its watery counter-part, will have many reversals, setbacks, failures, and losses. All of this movement is a natural progression in your evolving process of being an extraordinary sports parent. This is, in fact, the same process that your children experience. We are all in the same boat, so to speak, which is why we should have compassion for everyone's journey. At our best as sports parents, we acknowledge, trust, and accept this natural process. Without panic or fear, we allow our children to grow at their own pace and when they are ready. Without panic or fear, we allow ourselves to learn and grow at our own pace. As a parent of athletic kids, I am still learning. I experience setbacks and failures, and yet I continue moving forward because the ride is worth it. Both despite and because of the challenges, it has been an amazing, continual journey of growth, fulfillment, and joy.

With renewed enthusiasm and an open mind and heart, celebrate this gentle way of parenting athletes by embracing the pure spirit of playfulness. Take your first step and dive into this place of heart, this sacred space of right action. Have fun, laugh, and know that there is really no other purpose to this journey than to become more awakened to the beautiful give-and-take between you and your precious young athletes — this soulful dance of mindful, conscious sports parenting.

When you do things from your soul, you feel a river moving in you, a joy.

— Rumi

Acknowledgments

I t takes a small village to write and publish a good book. At this time in my literary career, I am well aware that I do not write books; I cowrite and rewrite them with the generous giving and love of other key players along the way. As I look back and connect the dots of this journey, I remain mindful of how fortunate I am to continue making a difference in the lives of others through my writing. And I also am very much aware that my work is not all of my doing. The "dots" listed below are the indispensable parties who helped make this book a reality.

Dot number one is my wife and life partner, Jan, who consistently reminded me that I had something valuable to offer and that I must, must write this book. After many such conversations,

I gave in and agreed that she was right. I love you, Jan, for strongly pushing me in this direction.

Caroline Pincus is dot number two. Caroline, an amazing book-publishing "midwife" with a heart of gold, read my proposal, convinced me that I had something worthwhile, and strongly suggested that I find a good agent to help me land a worthy publisher for my important manuscript. I am so grateful for you, Caroline, for this insightful advice.

I then contacted the inspiring, empowering literary agent Barbara Moulton, who became dot number three. Recommended by Caroline to work with me during this gestation period, Barbara helped position my manuscript for the best possible outcome. With her teacher's heart and lively warrior's spirit, she believed in me and the importance of my message for the masses. It didn't hurt that she happens to be a parent of athletic kids who coaches youth soccer part-time. Within a few weeks of contacting publishers, she found three houses that expressed deep interest in my manuscript. Because of Barbara, my writing and publishing work has discovered new, refreshing light. Barbara, I am eternally grateful for you and look forward to many more books together.

Then there is dot number four. Of the three interested publishers, I intuitively knew that senior editor Jason Gardner at New World Library was someone I could easily work with to make this a very special book. Barbara spoke highly of him, and I love that he is involved in youth sports as a parent. Jason, your gentle, kind, yet strong shepherding as you continually nudged me in creative directions has brought more vitality to this book — and, in the process, brought me much joy and taught me a lot. I appreciate your astute suggestions, your respectful tone, and your trust in my expertise along the way to completion. You're the best.

Dot number five is copy editor Jeff Campbell. He's the person who did all the heavy lifting, shaping my manuscript into the book that you are reading. I am so fortunate to have had such a wordsmith teaching me how to kick my writing up a few notches while he pruned every sentence with zeal. Honestly, Jeff, you've made me look much better as a writer at a time when I still have much to learn.

Dot number six is my office assistant and typist extraordinaire Sally Vaughn. Her suggestions, keen observations, and timely comments have been an enormous contribution to this book's readiness. I am grateful for her awesome input.

Of course, let me extend my gratefulness to thousands of sports parents — collectively, dot number seven — for encouraging, inspiring, empowering, and teaching me through their failures and successes much of what I need to know, what we all must learn in order to be at the top of our game for our little athletes.

Simply stated, if it hadn't been for these dots, there would be no book. Thank goodness for such awesome, helpful friends.

About the Author

While most consider him a sports psychologist, Dr. Jerry Lynch is also a coach, mentor, and teacher who guides and coaches athletes and parents to explore the meaning and purpose of sport, which is a powerful vehicle to help us understand the mental, emotional, and spiritual components of the bigger game called life. In the process of this exploration, overall athletic performance is greatly enhanced.

Dr. Lynch has a deep calling, one where he measures success not by "making a living" but rather by "making a difference" in the athletic and personal lives of those he works with. He helps others to understand how sport is a microcosmic classroom for helping athletes, coaches, and parents of sports kids develop the crucial capacities and virtues so absolutely essential to extraordinary performance in athletics and life: namely, to love, respect, and care for one another while simultaneously learning to enhance the spiritual elements of courage, commitment, patience, persistence, perseverance, sacrifice, integrity, trust, belief, and selflessness.

Dr. Lynch has been recognized as one of the top five in his profession nationwide. He is the former sports psychologist for various men's and women's sports teams — including basketball, lacrosse, field hockey, and soccer — at the universities of North Carolina, Maryland, and California, along with Boston, Duke, Syracuse, and Stanford Universities. Over the past twenty-five years of his forty-year career in athletics, he has worked with thirty-six national and world championship teams, and several of his clients have participated in various summer and winter Olympic Games. Most recently, he has established a consultancy with Steve Kerr, head coach of the world champion Golden State Warriors.

Dr. Lynch is a well-known and in-demand public speaker at leadership, coaching, athletic, and corporate conventions, and he presents clinics and workshops nationwide for coaches, sports parents, and athletes in college and high school. Some of his presentations include keynote talks at the New Zealand Academy of Sport, Der Deutsche Schmerztag in Germany, the National Field Hockey Coaches Association convention, the Ironman Sports Medicine Conference in Hawaii, the US Lacrosse national conventions, and the Nike/China Leadership Summit in Lanai, Hawaii.

Dr. Lynch has had extensive media coverage. He's been interviewed on national TV programs for CBS, NBC, and PBS, as well as featured in the *New York Times*, *Oprah Magazine*, *Sports Illustrated*, the *Baltimore Sun*, *Outside* magazine, and on over seventy-five national radio broadcasts, podcasts, and webinars.

Dr. Lynch received his doctorate in psychology from Penn State University, and he has done extensive postdoctoral work in the area of Eastern philosophy, Native American traditions, comparative religions, leadership development, and performance enhancement. He has been a national-class athlete, having been a member of a national championship team, and to this day he continues to train and compete in running and cycling. He has coached at the high school level as well as for Amateur Athletic Union (AAU) sports.

He is the author of twelve books, which have been translated into as many as ten languages, on coaching, parenting, mentoring, leadership, spirituality of sport, warrior spirit, peak performance, and sports psychology. He has nine DVDs on performance and coaching as well as two six-CD audio sets entitled *Performance in Athletics.*

Dr. Lynch is the founder and director of Way of Champions, a performance consulting group geared toward helping others master the inner game for peak performance in athletics and develop the essential spiritual qualities so necessary for the game of life. He maintains a private practice and an extensive sports psychology consultation service for athletes, coaches, and sports parents around the world. His book *Let Them Play* is the foundational guide for all of his nationwide clinics for parents of young athletes.

Jerry is the father of four high-energy, athletic children. He divides his time between his offices in Santa Cruz, California, and Boulder, Colorado, where he continues to train, run, bike, work, and write in the spirit of what he teaches and coaches.

Visit his website at www.wayofchampions.com or contact him via email: wayofchampions@gmail.com.